YOUR
Best Life
NOW

JOURNAL

YOUR
Best Life
NOW

JOURNAL

A GUIDE TO
REACHING YOUR
FULL POTENTIAL

JOEL OSTEEN

WARNER
Faith®

NEW YORK BOSTON NASHVILLE

Scripture quotations noted NASB are from the NEW AMERICAN STANDARD BIBLE®. Copyright © 1960, 1962, 1963, 1968, 1971, 1972, 1973, 1975, 1977, 1995 by The Lockman Foundation. Used by permission.

Scripture quotations noted NIV are from the HOLY BIBLE, NEW INTERNATIONAL VERSION®. Copyright © 1973, 1978, 1984 by International Bible Society. Used by permission of Zondervan Publishing House. All rights reserved.

Scripture quotations noted THE MESSAGE are from THE MESSAGE. Copyright © 1993, 1994, 1995, 1996, 2000, 2001, 2002. Used by permission of NavPress Publishing Group.

Scripture quotations noted TLB are from The Living Bible, copyright © 1971. Used by permission of Tyndale House Publishers, Inc., Wheaton, Illinois 60189. All rights reserved.

Scripture quotations noted NLT are from the Holy Bible, New Living Translation, copyright © 1996. Used by permission of Tyndale House Publishers, Inc., Wheaton, Illinois 60189. All rights reserved.

Scripture quotations noted NKJV are from THE NEW KING JAMES VERSION. Copyright © 1979, 1980, 1982, Thomas Nelson, Inc., Publishers.

Warner Faith
Time Warner Book Group
1271 Avenue of the Americas, New York, NY 10020
Visit our Web site at www.twbookmark.com.

The Warner Faith name and logo are registered trademarks of Time Warner Book Group.

Printed in the United States of America
First edition: April 2005
10 9 8 7 6 5 4 3

ISBN 0-446-57784-7

Book design by Charles Sutherland

PRESENTED TO

_____

BY

_____

OCCASION

_____

CONTENTS

Step Three: Discover the Power of Your Thoughts and Words

Step Four: Let Go of the Past

Step Five: Find Strength Through Adversity

STEP SIX: LIVE TO GIVE

STEP SEVEN: CHOOSE TO BE HAPPY

INTRODUCTION

Millions of people are discovering what it means to live "your best life now."

The secret is not really a secret at all. Happy, successful, fulfilled individuals understand that the future begins with what happens today. They make the most of the present moment and build their future one day at a time.

You can, too, and this book will help you do it.

Your Best Life Now Journal is divided into seven sections based on my bestselling book, *Your Best Life Now*. Ideally, this journal is intended to be used over the next seven weeks, one section per week. Each section comprises seven days' worth of bite-sized chunks of material that you can digest and respond to. Don't try to read the entire book in one sitting. Take your time and allow yourself to reflect on each day's material. During the next seven weeks, you will discover yourself adopting the key principles and beginning to live "your best life now." Although it would be extremely helpful to read the original book, it is not absolutely necessary to do so before using this journal. Throughout these pages, I'll remind you of the material in the main book by providing some condensed excerpts that we'll use as springboards for thought and reflection.

This journal is an invitation to do just that—to think and to reflect. It's an open door to self-discovery, so step through and begin the journey toward living the life you were born to live.

Explore what it means to enlarge your vision. Learn what God has to say about you and then rebuild your self-image according to His perspective. Understand the power of your thoughts and words. Begin to shake off the past. Renew your strength despite the pressures and adversities of the present. Learn to live as a giver, one who gives generously without reservations. And choose happiness each day.

No matter where you are or what challenges you are facing, you can have a life filled with satisfaction, peace, joy, and enthusiasm—not just for a day, or a week, but for the rest of your life!

HOW TO USE THIS BOOK

This book is meant to be written in. Underline important ideas within these pages, write yourself little notes of encouragement in the margins as you read, and jot down fresh ideas that come to you as you experience *Your Best Life Now*.

In this journal, you'll find thought-provoking questions, encouraging Scriptures, and simple prayers to help you focus your heart and mind on living today to the fullest. You will also find plenty of space to respond to what you're reading. Take some time to reflect on the stories. Ponder the questions. Allow the Scriptures to speak to you. Be still and listen to what God is saying through these words. Then write down your thoughts, your questions, your prayers, and your dreams. Many of your responses will involve your personal feelings, concerns, experiences, and areas of your life in which you want to improve.

Obviously, you could answer the questions mentally and then quickly move on to the next subject, but to get the maximum benefit from this journal, you'll find it extremely helpful to put your answers on paper. As you record your responses, you will begin to think through why you feel and believe the way you do. More important, you will have a written record of some matters about which God may be speaking to you concerning your attitudes and actions. And you'll have a record of your response to Him!

When you write your responses, be as honest as possible. Don't be afraid to freely express your thoughts and feelings. Don't worry about spelling or grammar or sentence structure. Attempt to get your "heart" on paper. Don't try to impress anyone with your answers. No teacher or critic is looking over your shoulder, waiting to correct you if you record the wrong response. In fact, since most of your responses are simply reflections of your own thoughts and feelings, they can't be considered "right" or "wrong." No tests will be given at the end of the book; this is one course you can be sure you will pass with flying colors!

When you use this journal, I suggest that you find a quiet, comfortable place where you can be free to express yourself without interruption. Allow yourself plenty of time to read each section carefully, and then thoughtfully respond to the material. Especially seek God's help and guidance regarding areas in which He may want to change you. Create in your own words a faith-building reminder of your journey to a new way of life—the life you were meant to live.

Let this journal stand as a testimony to the transforming power of God at work in you, a record of how you are learning to live "Your Best Life Now"!

—Joel Osteen

STEP ONE:

Enlarge Your Vision

DAY 1:

CHANGE YOUR MIND;
EXPAND YOUR WORLD

KEY TRUTH: To live your best life now, you must begin looking at life through eyes of faith, visualizing the life you want to live.

FROM THE TIME SHE WAS A LITTLE GIRL, TARA HOLLAND dreamed of becoming Miss America. After two years as runner-up in the Miss Florida pageant, she was tempted to give up, but she chose instead to focus on her goal. She rented videos of every pageant she could find—local pageants, state pageants, Miss Teen, Miss Universe, Miss World—and watched them over and over again.

As Tara watched each young woman crowned a winner, she pictured herself in that situation. She pictured herself receiving the crown. She pictured herself walking down the runway in victory. Time and time again she envisioned herself winning.

So when Tara was crowned Miss America in 1997, taking that long walk down the runway came as natural to her as breathing. Afterward, a reporter asked if she was nervous about being on television, in front of millions, accepting her crown. "No," she said, "I wasn't nervous at all. You see, I had walked down that runway thousands of times before." She was simply living out the dream, the vision, she had practiced so many times in her mind.

CONSIDER THIS: What about you? Have you ever imagined yourself accomplishing your dreams? Do you keep that vision of victory in front of you? How do you most often see and describe yourself—in terms of past experiences, present limitations, or future successes? Do you most often envision yourself winning or losing, succeeding or failing?

If you've packed away your dreams, dare to unpack them in the following space. Write down two lifelong dreams that prior to now, you haven't been able to imagine fulfilling. Dare to ask God to rekindle those dreams in your heart and mind. Describe what your life might look like when those dreams begin coming true:

Nothing can be done without hope and optimism.

—*Helen Keller*

> If you hear a voice telling you
> that you cannot paint, then
> by all means paint, and that
> voice will be silenced.
>
> —*Vincent Van Gogh*

WHAT THE SCRIPTURES SAY

Kindle afresh the gift of God which is in you.

—*2 Timothy 1:6 NASB*

"I know the plans I have for you," declares the LORD. "Plans to prosper you and not to harm you, plans to give you hope and a future."

—*Jeremiah 29:11 NIV*

A PRAYER FOR TODAY

Heavenly Father, You have given me eyes to see and a mind to search for wisdom. Today I ask that You open the eyes of my heart and my mind to see myself as You see me—blessed, loved, and full of joy! Help me to envision the dreams I've pushed aside, to see myself accepting and living out what You desire in my life.

Whether you believe you can do a thing or not, you are right.

—*Henry Ford*

TAKEAWAY TRUTH: Today, create an environment of faith and success by getting rid of negative, wrong thinking and replacing those thoughts and attitudes with a fresh vision of what your future can be. Do your best to reject thoughts of limitations and failure in your mind, and replace them with the empowering words of truth, victory, health, joy, peace, and happiness.

DAY 2:

OUT WITH THE OLD,
IN WITH THE NEW YOU

KEY TRUTH: Get rid of those old wineskins. Get beyond the barriers of the past and start expecting God to do great things in your life.

CENTURIES AGO, WINE WAS STORED IN LEATHER WINESKINS rather than bottles. Animal skins were dried and cured until the leather could be shaped into containers to hold the wine. When the wineskins were new, they were soft and pliable, but as they aged, they often lost their elasticity. They would become hardened and set, and they couldn't expand. If a person poured new wine into an old wineskin, the container would burst and the wine would be lost.

Interestingly, when Jesus wanted to encourage His followers to enlarge their visions, He reminded them, "You can't put new wine into old wineskins" (see Matthew 9:17).

Jesus was saying that you cannot have a larger life with restricted attitudes. That lesson is still relevant today. We are set in our ways, bound by our perspectives, and stuck in our thinking. God is trying to do something new, but unless we're willing to change, unless we're willing to expand and enlarge our vision, we'll miss His opportunities for us.

CONSIDER THIS: In Isaiah 43:19, God says, "Behold I am doing a new thing! . . . Do you not perceive and know it?" (AMP). God is always ready to do new things in our lives. He's trying to promote us, to increase us, to give us more. Yet, it's interesting that God asked the question, "Do you not perceive and know it?" In other words, are you making room for it in your own thinking? In the space below, write about some of the old cobweb-thinking that has kept you from perceiving a positive future—those old wineskins that are holding you back from perceiving God's best:

_____

_____

_____

———— ✧ ————

There is no sadder sight than
a young pessimist.

—*Mark Twain*

_____

_____

_____

Now, read back over your last journal entry and replace those old "wineskins" with new, hope-filled expectations of how you want to see God at work in your life:

_____

_____

_____

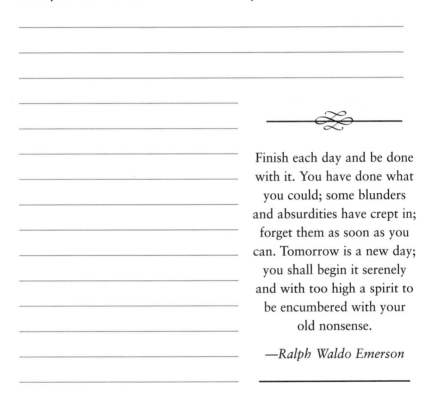

Finish each day and be done with it. You have done what you could; some blunders and absurdities have crept in; forget them as soon as you can. Tomorrow is a new day; you shall begin it serenely and with too high a spirit to be encumbered with your old nonsense.

—*Ralph Waldo Emerson*

WHAT THE SCRIPTURES SAY

Jesus said, "If you can believe, all things are possible."
—*Mark 9:23* NKJV

I pray also . . . that you may know the hope to which he has called you, the riches of his glorious inheritance in the saints, and his incomparably great power for us who believe.

—*Ephesians 1:18–19* NIV

A PRAYER FOR TODAY

Lord, that seed of hope You've placed in me is trying to take root. Give me the strength to clear away any weeds or rubble (those old wineskins) that might get in the way of this new thing You're doing. Bring on the sunshine, and allow just the right amount of rain, too. Expand my horizons, so this hope will grow and bring forth a tremendous harvest in my life.

If you have accomplished all that you have planned for yourself, you have not planned enough.

—*Meggido Message*

TAKEAWAY TRUTH: Don't settle for a small view of God. We serve the God that created the universe. Get rid of that small-minded view and begin to think as God thinks. Think big. Think increase. Think abundance. Think more than enough!

DAY 3:

GREAT EXPECTATIONS

KEY TRUTH: God usually meets us at our level of expectancy.

OUR EXPECTATIONS SET THE BOUNDARIES FOR OUR LIVES. JESUS said, "According to your faith will it be done to you" (Matthew 9:29 NIV). One translation puts it simply, "Have what your faith expects."

Some people tend to expect the worst. They go around with that "poor-old-me mentality," always negative, always depressed. "God, why don't You do something about my situation?" they grouse. "This is not fair!" They have what their faith expects.

Other people honestly feel so overwhelmed by their troubles, they have difficulty believing that anything good could happen to them. You hear them saying things such as, "Oh, I've got so many problems. My marriage is in trouble. My children won't do right. My business isn't doing well. My health is going downhill. How can I live with enthusiasm? How do you expect me to get up and say this is going to be a good day, when I have this big mess on my hands?"

Friend, that's what faith is all about. You have to start believing that good things are coming your way, and they will!

CONSIDER THIS: What are you expecting in life? Are you a "glass half empty" person or a "glass half full" person? Write your answer below and include how or why you came to have these expectations, for better or worse.

_____

_____

_____

———————❦———————

Many a losing entry has had
every attribute except one:
the belief he was going
to win.

—*Grantland Rice*

WHAT THE SCRIPTURES SAY

Set your minds and keep them set on what is above (the higher things).

—*Colossians 3:2* AMP

Faith is being sure of what we hope for and certain of what we do not see.

—Hebrews 11:1 NIV

A PRAYER FOR TODAY

God, I know that You are in control, even though I'm facing challenges today in my life. I know today could be the day that things turn around. Today could be the day that financial problems melt away. Today could be the day that relationships are restored. Today could be the day sick and hurting people are healed. Lord, I believe in miracles, and I know that even if I can't always see them with these human eyes, You are performing them even now. And I thank You for that. (*Continue this prayer by writing about your own specific circumstances below.*)

I like dreams of the future better than history of the past.

—Thomas Jefferson

———————————

The most rewarding things
you do in life are often the
ones that look like they
cannot be done.

—*Arnold Palmer*

TAKEAWAY TRUTH: Begin reprogramming your mind today: Start believing that things are going to change for the better, not because you deserve it, but simply because God loves you that much! It's a spiritual principle as well as a psychological fact: We move toward that which we see in our minds. If you can't see it, it is not likely to come to pass in your life.

DAY 4:

BEYOND BELIEF

KEY TRUTH: What you will receive is directly connected to how you believe.

I HEARD AN OLD STORY ABOUT A LITTLE FROG THAT WAS BORN at the bottom of a small, circular well, similar to those you might see at a typical rural farm. He and his family lived there, and he was content to play in the water, swimming all around that little well. He thought, *Life doesn't get any better than this. I have all that I need.*

But one day, he looked up and noticed the light at the top of the well. The little frog became curious, and wondered what was up there. Slowly, he climbed up the side of the well. When he got to the top, he cautiously peered out over the edge. Lo and behold, the first thing he saw was a pond. He couldn't believe it. It was a thousand times bigger than the well. He ventured farther and discovered a huge lake. He stood there gazing in amazement. Eventually, the little frog hopped a long way and came to the ocean, where everywhere he looked, all he could see was water. He was shocked beyond measure. He began to realize how limited his thinking had been. He thought he had it all back in the well, but all he really had was a drop in the bucket compared to what God wanted him to enjoy.

So many times we're like that little frog. Each of us enclosed in our own little well, the comfortable environment in which we were raised. It's all we've ever known—a certain level of living, a certain way of thinking. All the while, God has so much more in store for us. God's dream for our lives is so much bigger, so much greater than we can imagine. If God showed us everything He had in store for us, it would boggle our minds.

CONSIDER THIS: God is a progressive God. He wants you to go further than your parents ever went. He wants you to be the one to break the mold. Maybe you were raised in a negative environment. Everybody around you was negative and critical, depressed, down in the dumps, and discouraged. No doubt, you're tempted to use your negative upbringing as an excuse to live the same way. But you can be the person to change your family tree! You don't have to keep that negative cycle going. You can be the one to break the curse in your family. You can be the one to raise the bar. You can affect future generations by the decisions you make today.

Write down three "bigger than life" dreams, goals, or plans for your life. Then write three specific actions you can take today to help make those dreams become realities:

_____

_____

_____

_____

_____

———

There are those who look at things the way they are, and ask why . . . I dream of things that never were, and ask why not?

—*Robert F. Kennedy*

WHAT THE SCRIPTURES SAY

I know what I'm doing. I have it all planned out—plans to take care of you, not abandon you, plans to give you the future you hope for.

—*Jeremiah 29:11* THE MESSAGE

Hope that is seen is no hope at all. Who hopes for what he already has?

—*Romans 8:24* NIV

A PRAYER FOR TODAY

Lord, You already know all the negative thoughts and limitations that run through my mind. But I've had enough of them, and with Your help, I'm going to break this cycle of mediocrity; I reject a "this is the best I can do" mentality. I believe You have great plans for me, and I want to fulfill my destiny. Thank You for believing in me!

———— ✥ ————

Whatever you can do or
dream you can, begin it.
Boldness has genius, power,
and magic in it.

—*Johann Wolfgang von
Goethe [1749–1832]*

TAKEAWAY TRUTH: Today, I will not settle for mediocrity. I will not be limited by my past history, my present circumstances, or by anything that I feel I lack in my life. God is my source, and God is not limited. I will trust in Him and His unlimited resources.

DAY 5:

UN-MAKE-UP YOUR MIND

KEY TRUTH: If you will change your thinking, God can change your life.

EVERY FOUR YEARS, THE WORLD'S ATTENTION TURNS TO THE summer Olympic games. Watching the summer games nowadays, it is almost difficult to remember that only a few decades ago, track-and-field experts pompously declared that no runner would be able to break the four-minute mile barrier. Ostensibly, a human being couldn't run that far, that fast, for that length of time. "Experts" conducted all sorts of profound studies to show how impossible it was to beat the four-minute barrier. And for years, they were right. Nobody ran a mile in less than four minutes.

But someone forgot to tell Roger Bannister. Even if they had, he wouldn't have believed the experts anyway. He didn't dwell on the impossibilities. He began to train, believing he was going to break that record. Sure enough, he went out one day and made sports history, breaking the four-minute mile barrier. He did what the experts said couldn't be done.

Now, here is what I find so interesting about Roger's story: Within ten years, 336 other runners had broken the four-minute-mile record, as well! Think about that. For hundreds of years, as far back as statisticians kept track-and-field records, nobody was able to run a mile in less than four minutes. For years, runners believed it was impossible. But then within a decade, more than three hundred people from various geographic locations were able to do it. What happened? Simple. The barrier was in their minds.

CONSIDER THIS: You can't go around thinking thoughts of defeat and failure and expect God to fill you with joy, power, and victory. You can't go around thinking thoughts of poverty and lack, and expect God to fill you with abundance.

Have some determination; ask God to put some fire in your spirit. Begin speaking in terms of victory rather than defeat. Your words have amazing power, so quit talking about what you can't do, and start talking about what God *can* do. Keep your mind focused on God's goodness.

Write out below some of the ways God has been good to you. You probably won't have room for everything, but that's okay. List just a few of the good things God has done for you. Take a moment to thank Him while you're at it.

I want to know God's
thoughts. The rest are details.

—*Albert Einstein*

_____

_____

——————⸎——————

Guard well thy thoughts; our
thoughts are heard in heaven.

—*Owen D. Young*

_____

Now, list some things that you believe God still wants to do
in your life. Be specific and boldly express your faith; don't be
bashful. Write about what God can do in and through you, not
merely what you can do on your own:

_____

_____

_____

_____

——————⸎——————

The trouble with most people
is that they think with their
hopes or fears or wishes
rather than with their minds.

—*Walter Duranty*

WHAT THE SCRIPTURES SAY

Enlarge your house; build an addition; spread out your home! For you soon will be bursting at the seams.

—*Isaiah 54:2–3* NLT

Little children, you are of God [you belong to Him] and have [already] defeated and overcome them [the agents of the antichrist], because He Who lives in you is greater (mightier) than he who is in the world.

—*1 John 4:4* AMP

A PRAYER FOR TODAY

Lord Jesus, break down the strongholds of _____ [*tell God the specifics*] in my thought-life. Clean house in my stubborn mind, and sweep away all the clutter that keeps me from believing in You to accomplish the best in my life. Not just pretty good or even real good, but the absolute best. Put a fire in my spirit, Lord. Help me to stop looking behind me or to the side. Help me to focus only on You and Your goodness in my life.

TAKEAWAY TRUTH: For a long time, my mind has been packed wall-to-wall with negative, limiting thoughts. But today I'm beginning to change my mind, to allow God to help me make it anew. No more limitations. God created me to be a champion in life, and I'm going to start thinking like a champion.

DAY 6:

DISCOVERING THE VIP WITHIN

KEY TRUTH: It's not who you are, but *whose* you are that counts. Because God is your heavenly Father, doors of opportunity will open for you.

ALL MY LIFE, I'VE BEEN AWARE OF GOD'S FAVOR. FROM THE time my siblings and I were little kids, every day before we left for school, our mother would pray, "Father, I thank You that Your angels have charge over my children, and that Your hand of favor will always be upon them."

Consequently—and I say this humbly—I've come to expect to be treated deferentially. I've learned to expect people to want to help me. My attitude is: I'm a child of the Most High God. My Father created the whole universe. He has crowned me with favor; therefore, I can expect preferential treatment. I can expect people to go out of their way to want to help me.

The Bible clearly states that God has "crowned us with glory and honor" (Psalm 8:5 NLT). The word *honor* could also be translated as "favor," and *favor* means "to assist, to provide with special advantages and to receive preferential treatment."

In other words, God wants to make your life easier. He wants to assist you, to promote you, to give you advantages. He wants you to receive preferential treatment. But if we're going to experience more of God's favor, we must live more "favor-minded." To be favor-minded simply means that we expect God's special help, and we are releasing our faith, knowing that God wants to assist us.

Please don't misinterpret what I'm saying. In no way should we ever be arrogant and think we are better than somebody else. But as God's children we can live with confidence and boldness, expecting good things. We can expect preferential treatment, not because of *who* we are, but because of *whose* we are. We can expect people to want to help us because of who our Father is.

CONSIDER THIS: God's favor surrounds you like a shield. It doesn't matter what the circumstances look like in your life. Regardless of how many people tell you it can't be done, if you'll persevere, declaring the favor of God and staying in an attitude of faith, God will open doors for you, and change circumstances on your behalf.

List three difficulties you're facing or worries you are currently struggling with. Then as you pray the prayer below, boldly declare God's favor in each of those situations.

_____

_____

_____

_____

_____

_____

_____

—————⚮—————

To one who has faith, no
explanation is necessary. To
one without faith, no
explanation is possible.

—*Thomas Aquinas*

WHAT THE SCRIPTURES SAY

You made us only a little lower than [the angels], and you crowned us with glory and honor.

—*Psalm 8:5* NLT

We know that all that happens to us is working for our good if we love God and are fitting into his plans.

—*Romans 8:28* TLB

A PRAYER FOR TODAY

Father, I thank You that I have Your favor. Your favor is opening doors of opportunity. Your favor is bringing success into my life. Your favor is causing people to want to help me. Help me go about my life in total confidence, expecting good things to happen.

So nigh is grandeur to our dust, so near is God to man, when Duty whispers low, *Thou must*, the youth replies, *I can!*

—*Ralph Waldo Emerson*

TAKEAWAY TRUTH: Today, I will be bold and declare God's favor upon my life, even in the mundane aspects of this day, and no matter what happens—or doesn't happen—I will believe that He is guiding and leading and moving on my behalf in every situation. I will do my part, and God will do His part. He is working in everything for my good.

DAY 7:

VIP 101: LIVING AS IF YOU BELIEVE IT

KEY TRUTH: Don't take God's favor for granted.

GOD WANTS TO HELP YOU IN EVERY AREA OF YOUR LIFE, NOT just the big matters. When you live favor-minded, you'll begin to see God's goodness in the everyday, ordinary details at the grocery store, at the ball field, the mall, at work, or at home. You may be stuck in traffic. The lane next to you is moving well, but you just can't get over there. Then, suddenly, for no apparent reason, somebody slows down and waves you in. That's the favor of God.

You may be at a grocery store in an extremely long checkout line, and you're in a hurry. Another checker taps you on the shoulder and says, "Come with me. I'm opening this additional register over here." That's the favor of God assisting you. The favor of God causes other people to extend preferential treatment to you.

You may be out to lunch when you "just happen" to bump into somebody you've been wanting to meet. Perhaps that person is someone you admire or hope to learn from, or possibly he or she is someone with whom you have been hoping to do business, but you couldn't get to him. That is not a coincidence. That's the favor of God causing you to be at the right place at the right time.

When these kinds of things happen, be grateful. Don't take God's favor for granted. Say, "Father, thank You for Your favor. Thank You for assisting me."

CONSIDER THIS: The Bible is replete with examples of people who were in great need when the favor of God came on them in a new way, and their situation turned around. Consider the trials of Noah, Ruth, Joseph, and Job. God granted special favor to these faithful men and women in times of flood, family struggles, mistreatment, and grief and loss. Nothing could keep them down.

The favor of God can bring you out of your difficulties and turn your adversities around for good, too. Are you ready to begin living as if you believe it? If not, what is standing in your way? Dare to declare God's favor in your situation. Pray something such as, "Father, I believe that I have Your favor today with my boss"; "I have Your favor in that business decision." Write some faith-filled statements expressing your heavenly Father's favor in specific situations you are facing.

_____

_____

_____

_____

_____

_____

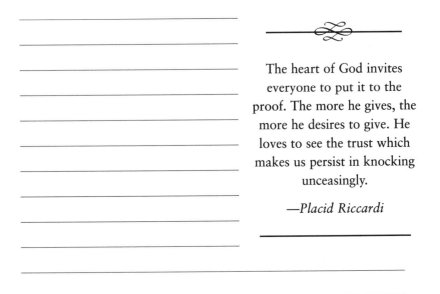

The heart of God invites everyone to put it to the proof. The more he gives, the more he desires to give. He loves to see the trust which makes us persist in knocking unceasingly.

—*Placid Riccardi*

WHAT THE SCRIPTURES SAY

Surely your goodness and unfailing love will pursue me all the days of my life, and I will live in the house of the LORD forever.

—*Psalm 23:6* NLT

Your beauty and love chase after me every day of my life.

—*Psalm 23:6* THE MESSAGE

Set your hope wholly and unchangeably on the grace (divine favor) that is coming to you.

—*1 Peter 1:13* AMP

A PRAYER FOR TODAY

Dear Father, I'm really beginning to believe what You've been saying all along: that You have granted me favor; that nothing is beyond my reach because You are the Source of all good things in my life. I may not understand it, I may not deserve it, but I pray I never take this honor, this grace, for granted. With Your help, I'm going to accept it and declare it boldly over every area of my life—big and small—and I'm never going to give it up! Thank You for loving me so passionately.

Faith is thinking something is true to the extent that we act on it.

—W. T. Purkiser

TAKEAWAY TRUTH: Today, nothing is going to keep me down because my hope is in God, the almighty Creator of heaven and earth.

STEP TWO:

Develop a Healthy Self-Image

DAY 1:

WILL THE REAL YOU
PLEASE STAND UP?

KEY TRUTH: You will never rise above the image you have of yourself in your own mind.

BY MOST STANDARDS, CARLY SHOULD NOT HAVE MADE IT. Overweight, with one leg slightly shorter than the other as the result of a childhood accident, Carly was the lone woman employed in a largely male-dominated field. She had to earn her right to be heard nearly every day. Some people laughed at her appearance or her halting walk, some made snide remarks behind her back, some were inconsiderate to her face, but Carly paid little attention. She knew who she was, and she knew she was good at what she did, so when other people attempted to put her down, she regarded them as having the problem. "Emotionally challenged," she often quipped about her detractors.

Despite the factors working against her, Carly continued to receive one promotion after another, eventually becoming the CEO of her company and a highly-sought-after expert in her field. How did she do it?

Carly's secret is her incredibly positive self-image. A devout Christian, Carly believes that she has been made in the image of God, and that He gives her life intrinsic value. She doesn't strive for the approval of other people, or depend on compliments from her superiors or peers to feel good about herself. Bright, friendly, articulate, and extremely competent in her work, Carly goes through life with a smile. While others shake their heads in amazement at her attitude, Carly is living her best life now!

CONSIDER THIS: Your *self-image* is much like a self-portrait; it is who and what you picture yourself to be. Do you base how you feel about yourself on false, fickle standards such as what neighborhood you live in, the style of car you drive, or the opinions of power-lunch groups? If so, your self-image may not be an accurate reflection of who you really are. Every person has an image of himself or herself. Who do you think you are?

Describe yourself below as you honestly see yourself, then at the bottom write out the question "But who does God say that I am?" Make special note in your journal of any differences of opinion that you discover between the way you see yourself and the way God regards you.

_____

_____

_____

_____

_____

_____

_____

_____

_____

_____

_____

_____   ❧

_____   That kind of life is most
                                  happy which affords us the
_____   most opportunities of gaining
                                  our own self-esteem.
_____
                                      —*Samuel Johnson*
_____

_____

WHAT THE SCRIPTURES SAY

He said to me, "My grace is sufficient for you, for my power
is made perfect in weakness." Therefore I will boast all the
more gladly about my weaknesses, so that Christ's power may
rest on me.

—*2 Corinthians 12:9* NIV

God abides in us, and His love has been perfected in us.

—*1 John 4:12* NKJV

A PRAYER FOR TODAY

Father God, I know I have to learn to love and accept myself
as Your beloved child. Help me to see myself as You see me.
Help me to know that Your love is unconditional, that it is
based not on what I do, but on who I am as Your child. Help

me, Lord, to be the person You created me to be—unique, confident, and victorious! I want to be that person, the real me!

_____

_____

_____

_____

_____

———————❧———————

If you're not beguiling by age twelve, forget it.

—*Lucy [Charles Schulz]*

TAKEAWAY TRUTH: True self-esteem is not based on what I think or feel about myself or what others think about me. True self-esteem can be based only on what God says about me. I am who He says I am.

DAY 2:

LET THAT GRASSHOPPER GO

KEY TRUTH: Don't focus on your weaknesses; focus on your God.

REMEMBER JOSHUA AND CALEB, TWO OF THE TEN SPIES MOSES sent to check out the opposition in the land of Canaan and get a feel for the land before battle?

The other eight came back and said, "It is indeed a land flowing with milk and honey, but we don't have a chance. We'll never defeat those people. They're too big and they're too strong." The mental image they had of themselves was as small, weak, defeated grasshoppers, ready to be squished, helpless before the giants opposing them. They came back with a negative report because they were focused on their circumstances. They lost the battle before it even started.

But Joshua and Caleb had a totally different report. They possessed the same data as their eight colleagues, but it was almost as though they had gone to a different place. "Moses, we are well able to possess the land," they said. "Yes, there are giants there, and the giants are formidable, but our God is much bigger. Yes, the people are strong, but our God is stronger. Because of Him, we are well able. Let's go in at once and possess the land."

CONSIDER THIS: God loves to use ordinary people just like you and me, faults and all, to do extraordinary things. You may not feel capable in your own strength, but that's okay. God's Word states that He always causes us to triumph. He expects us to live victoriously.

Learn to guard your mind, control your thought life, and begin to dwell on the good things of God. Don't allow your self-image to be shaped by nonbiblical concepts that are contrary to God's opinion of you. If you're always thinking about defeat, failure, how weak you are, or how impossible your circumstances look, then just as those ten spies in biblical times, you will develop a "grasshopper mentality."

You can complain because roses have thorns, or you can rejoice because thorns have roses.

—*Ziggy [Tom Wilson]*

_____

_____

_____

_____

_____

_____

_____

_____

_____

_____

> One important key to success is self-confidence. An important key to self-confidence is preparation.
>
> —*Arthur Ashe*

WHAT THE SCRIPTURES SAY

God said, "Let Us make man in Our image, according to Our likeness; and let them rule over the fish of the sea and over the birds of the sky and over the cattle and over all the earth" . . . God created man in His own image, in the image of God He created him; male and female He created them.

—*Genesis 1:26–27* NASB

What is man that You take thought of him, and the son of man that You care for him? Yet You have made him a little lower than God, and You crown him with glory and majesty!

—*Psalm 8:4–5* NASB

A PRAYER FOR TODAY

Father, I know that I am not a cosmic accident, wandering randomly and aimlessly through life. I know that you have a specific purpose for me. And yet, I admit that sometimes the struggles of my life have discouraged me to the point that I've simply accepted "this is the way it is." But that is a lie. Thank You, God, for the plans You've already made for me, plans to do the seemingly impossible. Help me to reprogram my mind with Your Word, to be a "can do" person, so that I'm ready to accept all You have in store for me.

He who limps is still walking.

—*Stanislaw J. Lec*

TAKEAWAY TRUTH: Today, I will reject that grasshopper mentality. I will believe what the Bible says about who I am.

DAY 3:

YOU: A GOD'S-EYE VIEW

KEY TRUTH: Learn to be happy with who God made you to be.

THE SCRIPTURE SAYS, "WE ARE GOD'S WORKMANSHIP." THE word *workmanship* implies that you are not yet a finished product; you are a "work in process." Throughout life, God is continually shaping and molding us into the people He wants us to be. The key to future success is to not become discouraged with your past or present while you are in the process of being "completed." Whether you realize it or not, right now God is moving you onward toward greater things.

When you are tempted to get discouraged, remind yourself that according to God's Word, your future is getting brighter; you are on your way to a new level of glory. You may think you've got a long way to go, but you need to look back at how far you've already come. You may not be everything you want to be, but at least you can thank God that you're not what you used to be.

Our individual value is intrinsic; it is not something we have earned, nor can we earn it. God built value into us when He created us. To God, we are His ultimate creations. That means you can stop obsessing about all your faults and give yourself a break. Every person has weaknesses. The great news is that God knows everything about you, both good and bad, and He still loves you and values you unconditionally. God does not always approve of our behavior. He is not pleased when we go against His will, and when we do, we always suffer the consequences and have to work with Him to correct our thoughts, words, actions, or attitudes. And while you should work to improve in the areas where you fall short, nothing you do will ever cause God to love you less . . . or more.

CONSIDER THIS: Imagine that I am handing you a new, crisp one-hundred-dollar bill. Would you want it? Suppose I crumpled it up and it wasn't quite as good-looking as it was the day it came from the mint. Would you still want it? Sure! But wait, what if I took it out in the parking lot, threw it on the ground, stomped on it until it the picture on the bill was barely perceptible. It's now dirty, stained, and soiled. Do you still want it? Of course.

That's the way God sees each one of us. We all go through challenges and struggles. Sometimes we feel like that hundred-dollar bill, all crumpled and soiled. But just as that hundred-dollar bill still has value, you will never, ever lose your value. Your value has been placed in you by the Creator of the universe, and nobody can take it away from you.

Do you see the intrinsic value that God has placed on your life? If so, describe what you see. If not, how do you see yourself? How does your description compare with the way God sees you?

God is our Creator. God
made us in his image and
likeness. Therefore we are
creators . . . the joy of
creativeness should be ours.

—*Dorothy Day*

WHAT THE SCRIPTURES SAY

The path of the righteous is like the light of dawn, that shines
brighter and brighter until the full day.

—*Proverbs 4:18* NASB

[God] brought me up out of a horrible pit, out of the miry clay,
and set my feet upon a rock, and established my steps. He has
put a new song in my mouth.

—*Psalm 40:2–3* NKJV

Although my father and my mother have forsaken me, yet the
Lord will take me up [adopt me as His child].

—*Psalm 27:10* AMP

A PRAYER FOR TODAY

Thank You, Father, for knowing how valuable I am and for telling me so in Your Word. Thank You for seeing my potential. I may not understand everything that's happening in my life right now, but I know You are in control. Your ways are better and higher than my ways. Even when everybody else rejects me, help me to remember that You always stand before me with open arms. Thank You, Father, for never giving up on me.

If you don't matter to you, it's hard to matter to others.

—*Malcolm Forbes*

TAKEAWAY TRUTH: I am made in the image of almighty God. He has crowned me with glory and honor. God considers me—ME!—His masterpiece!

DAY 4:

BELIEVING TODAY, BECOMING TOMORROW

KEY TRUTH: What *you* believe has a much greater impact on your life than what anyone else believes.

IT IS CRUCIAL THAT WE SEE OURSELVES AS GOD SEES US, SINCE we will never rise above the image we have of ourselves. If we see ourselves barely making it, always having problems, and never happy, we will subconsciously move toward that sort of life. To move forward in life, we must change our focus. We must believe.

Understand this: God will help you, but you cast the deciding vote. If you choose to stay focused on negative elements in your life, if you focus on what you can't do and what you don't have, then by your own choice you are agreeing to be defeated and conspiring with the enemy. You are opening the door and allowing destructive thoughts, words, actions, and attitudes to dominate your life.

Nobody can have faith for you. Certainly, other people can pray for you, they can believe for you, they can quote the Scriptures to you, but you must exercise faith for yourself. If you are always depending on somebody else to keep you happy, somebody else to encourage you or to get you out of trouble, you will live in perpetual weakness and disappointment. You must make a decision that you are going to be a believer. Take charge of your life and decide, "No matter what comes against me, I believe in God. I'm going to have a positive outlook for my life."

CONSIDER THIS: If you'll get into agreement with God, if you'll focus on your possibilities, your faith will enable God to show up and work supernaturally in your life. Your faith will help you overcome your obstacles and allow you to reach new levels of victory. But it's up to you. It depends on your outlook. Are you focused on your problems, or are you focused on your God?

Faith is taking the first step even when you don't see the whole staircase.

—*Martin Luther King Jr.*

WHAT THE SCRIPTURES SAY

[Jesus] touched their eyes and said, "Because of your faith, it will happen." And suddenly they could see!

—*Matthew 9:29* NLT

[God said to Abraham,] "I will bless you and make your name famous, and you will be a blessing to many others."

—*Genesis 12:2* TLB

A PRAYER FOR TODAY

Today, I claim the promise You made to Abraham, Lord, that You would bless him so that he would be a blessing to others. I am believing for all the great things You have for me: financial stability, strong relationships with those I love, peace in my family and joy in my life . . . (*Add your own list of great expectations here.*):

_____

_____

_____

_____

_____

_____

_____

_____

_____

You are the God of all goodness, and I believe that You will bring these blessings to pass in my life so that I can be a blessing in the lives of others. Thank You, Father, for what You are doing in my life.

The more we live and try to practice the Sermon on the Mount, the more shall we experience blessing.

—*David Martyn Lloyd-Jones*

TAKEAWAY TRUTH: I am what I am today because of what I believed about myself yesterday. And I will be tomorrow what I believe about myself right now.

DAY 5:

DARE TO BELIEVE FOR THE "IMPOSSIBLE"

KEY TRUTH: If you dare to see the invisible, God will do the impossible.

I LOVE THE OLD TESTAMENT ACCOUNT OF WHEN GOD TOLD Abraham that he and his wife, Sarah, were going to have a child even though they were close to one hundred years old. When Sarah heard the news, she laughed. She probably said, "Abraham, you've got to be kidding. I'm not going to have a baby. I'm too old. That's never going to happen to me. And besides, look at you. You're no spring chicken, either!"

Sarah didn't have the correct vision. The condition of her heart wasn't right. She couldn't see herself having that child; she couldn't conceive it in her heart.

And you probably recall the story. Year after year went by, and Abraham and Sarah had no children. After a while, they decided to "help" God fulfill His promise. Sarah told Abraham to sleep with her maid, Hagar. The two of them conceived and gave birth to a child named Ishmael. But that wasn't God's best.

God wanted to give Sarah a baby, one that she gave birth to herself.

Still more years went by, and no child. Finally, Sarah became pregnant. What changed? God's promise was the same all along. I'm convinced that the key to the promise coming to pass was that Sarah finally conceived it in her heart and then she was able to conceive in her physical body. She had to believe she could become pregnant before she actually became with child.

Nearly twenty years after God spoke the promise, little Isaac was born to Abraham and Sarah. And I believe the main reason why he wasn't born sooner, one of the major delays in the fulfillment of the promise, was simply the fact that Sarah couldn't conceive it in her heart. She couldn't see it through her eyes of faith. She couldn't believe for the impossible.

CONSIDER THIS: Stop focusing on what you can't do and start focusing on what God can do. The Bible says, "The things which are impossible with men are possible with God" (Luke 18:27 NKJV). Let that seed take root inside you. Divide the journal space below into two columns by drawing a line down the middle of the page. On the left, list some of the "impossibilities" in your life; on the right, write out what God is capable of doing in that situation.

_____

_____

_____

_____

_____

_____

_____

_____

_____

_____

> Every calling is great when greatly pursued.
>
> —*Oliver Wendell Holmes Jr.*

WHAT THE SCRIPTURES SAY

He who began a good work in you will carry it on to completion until the day of Christ Jesus.

—*Philippians 1:6* NIV

Put on the full armor of God, so that when the day of evil comes, you may be able to stand your ground.

—*Ephesians 6:13* NIV

"My thoughts are not your thoughts, neither are your ways my ways," declares the LORD.

—*Isaiah 55:8* NIV

A PRAYER FOR TODAY

Dear Father, help me to live with faith and expectancy, to turn over the situations in my life to You and trust you to take care of every detail. You can do all things. Your ways are higher and better than anything I can imagine, and I know You are not limited to the natural world. You can move heaven and earth, if You so choose. I believe with all my heart that You can make my dreams, my hopes, my goals more than possible. You can make them reality. Thank You, God, for doing the impossible in my life!

_____

_____

_____

_____

> You cannot plan the future by the past.
>
> —*Edmund Burke*

TAKEAWAY TRUTH: I don't have to figure out how God is going to solve my problem. I don't have to understand how He's going to bring it to pass. That's His responsibility. My job is to simply believe that He will.

DAY 6:

PUT DOWN THE CHEESE AND CRACKERS!

KEY TRUTH: Don't settle for anything less than God's best.

YEARS AGO, BEFORE TRANSATLANTIC FLIGHT WAS COMMON, A man wanted to travel from Europe to the United States. He worked hard, saved every extra penny he could, and finally had just enough money to purchase a ticket aboard a cruise ship. The trip across the ocean at that time required about two or three weeks. He went out and bought a suitcase and filled it full of cheese and crackers. That's all he could afford.

Once on board, all the other passengers went to the large, ornate dining room to eat their gourmet meals. Meanwhile, the poor man would go over in the corner and eat his cheese and crackers. This went on day after day. He could smell the delicious food being served in the dining room. How he longed to join them, but he had no extra money.

Toward the end of the trip, another man came up to him and said, "Sir, I can't help but notice that you are always over there eating those cheese and crackers at mealtimes. Why don't you come into the banquet hall and eat with us?"

The traveler's face flushed with embarrassment. "Well, to tell you the truth, I had only enough money to buy the ticket. I don't have any extra money to purchase fancy meals."

The other passenger raised his eyebrows in surprise. He shook his head and said, "Sir, don't you realize the meals are included in the price of the ticket? Your meals have already been paid for!"

CONSIDER THIS: Every moment we go around with that "weak worm of the dust" mentality, we're eating more cheese and crackers. Every time we shrink back and say, "I can't do it; I don't have what it takes," we're eating more cheese and crackers instead of the gourmet meals available to us.

God has prepared a fabulous banquet for you, complete with everything you need—joy, forgiveness, restoration, peace, healing—waiting for you, already paid for. You may have gone through some great disappointments in life, but you are a child of the Most High God. Having some things go wrong in your life does not change who you are. If one dream dies, dream another dream.

What is holding you back from God's banquet table? What is standing in your way? What practical steps can you take to show that you are ready to stop settling for less than God's best?

_____

_____

_____

_____

_____

_____

_____

_____   ——————⊰⊱——————

_____

_____   The difference between
                                                 perseverance and obstinacy is
_____   that one comes from a strong
                                                 will, and the other from a
_____   strong won't.

_____   —*Henry Ward Beecher*

_____

_____

_____

_____

_____

WHAT THE SCRIPTURES SAY

We are more than conquerors!

—*Romans 8:38*

[God] gives power to the weak, and to those who have no might
He increases strength.

—*Isaiah 40:29* NKJV

A PRAYER FOR TODAY

Dear Father, I am so grateful for Your mercy and grace in my
life, and yet I still try to hang on to that cheese and those

cracker crumbs, thinking it's too good to be true, too much to forgive, too much to restore. I humbly ask You to take my insecurities and fears and guilt and shame and remove them as Your Word says You remove confessed sin—as far as the east is from the west. I want to sit at the table You have prepared for me. Please open the doors, Lord. I'm coming in!

Try *claiming* God's blessings instead of merely *longing* for them.

—*Henry Jacobsen*

TAKEAWAY TRUTH: I don't have to live in guilt and condemnation any longer; I don't have to go through life worried and full of fear. The price for an abundant life has been paid. My freedom is included in my ticket if I'll just rise up and take my place.

DAY 7:

EMBRACEABLE, ORIGINAL YOU

KEY TRUTH: Be the best you can be, then you can feel good about yourself.

YOU CAN DARE TO BE HAPPY WITH WHO YOU ARE RIGHT NOW and accept yourself, faults and all. A lot of people don't realize it, but the root cause of many of their social, physical, and emotional problems is simply the fact that they don't like themselves. They are uncomfortable with how they look, how they talk, or how they act. They are always comparing themselves with other people, wishing they were something different. "If I just had his personality . . ." "If I looked like she looks." "If my thighs just weren't so big." "If I had less here and more somewhere else, then I'd be happy."

No, you can be happy with who God made you to be, and quit wishing you were something different. If God wanted you to look like a fashion model, a movie star or a famous athlete, or anyone else, He would have made you look like them. If God wanted you to have a different personality, He would have given you that personality. Don't compare yourself to other people; learn to be happy with who God made you to be.

CONSIDER THIS: God went to great lengths to make sure each of us is an original. We should not feel badly because our personality, tastes, hobbies, or even spiritual proclivities are not the same as another person's. Some people are outgoing and energetic; other people are more timid and laid-back. Some people like to wear suits and ties; other people are more comfortable wearing blue jeans. Some people close their eyes and lift their hands when they worship God; others worship God in a more subdued manner. And guess what? God likes it all! God loves variety.

In the space below, list some of the qualities or characteristics that make you unique. Write what you like about yourself: your gifts, talents, spiritual and physical attributes, hobbies, or personality traits.

_____

_____

Millions long for immortality
who don't know what to do
on a rainy Sunday afternoon.

—Susan Ertz

_____

_____

_____

_____

_____

_____

_____

_____

_____

WHAT THE SCRIPTURES SAY

Each one should test his own actions. Then he can take pride in himself, without comparing himself to somebody else, for each one should carry his own load.

—*Galatians 6:4–5* NIV

I know the LORD is always with me. I will not be shaken, for he is right beside me.

—*Psalm 16:8* NLT

A PRAYER FOR TODAY

Lord, You know my weaknesses, those areas in my life and in my mind where I struggle to believe. I praise You for continuing to refine those areas, sharpening my mind and strengthening my heart to beat like Yours. Thank You for making me, me. Help me to realize what a treasure I am in Your eyes! Thank You for lavishing Your mercy, grace, and favor on my life. You alone are worthy of praise!

———— ✦ ————

There is a great man who
makes every man feel small.
But the really great man is
the man who makes every
man feel great.

—*G. K. Chesterton*

TAKEAWAY TRUTH: I will be confident in who I am. I'm
not going to go around pretending, wishing I were someone
else, trying to fit into everybody's mold. I am free to run my
own race.

STEP THREE:

Discover the Power of Your Thoughts and Words

DAY 1:

DIGGING A NEW RIVER

KEY TRUTH: When you think positive, excellent thoughts, you will be propelled toward greatness.

WHEN YOUR THOUGHTS HAVE BEEN RUNNING IN A CERTAIN pattern for a long period of time, it's as though you have been digging a deep riverbed, and the water can flow only in one direction. With every pessimistic thought, you dig that river a bit deeper. The flow accelerates, growing stronger as it goes. After a period of time, the water is flowing so strongly, every thought that comes out of the river is negative because that's the only way the water is flowing. You have programmed your mind into a negative thinking pattern.

Fortunately, it's possible to dig a new river, one going in a positive direction. The way to do so is by one thought at a time. When you dwell on God's Word and start seeing the best in situations, little by little, one thought at a time, you redirect the flow of that river. At first, just a little water will be redirected out of the negative stream and trickle over into that positive stream. It may not look like much at first, but as you continue to reject negative thoughts and redirect the flow, as you choose faith instead of fear, expecting good things, and take control of your thought life, that negative stream will dwindle and the positive river will flow with much greater force. If you'll keep it up, eventually that old negative river will dry up, and you will discover a whole new river flowing with positive, faith-filled thoughts of victory.

Let's be real. That river of negative thinking wasn't formed overnight, nor will it be redirected without some conscious, strenuous effort on your part. God will help you, but you are going to have to make quality decisions every day, choosing the good, rejecting the bad. Determine to keep your mind set on the good things of God.

Our thoughts contain tremendous power. Remember, we draw in to our lives that which we constantly think about. If we're always dwelling on the negative, then we will attract negative people, experiences, and attitudes. If we're always dwelling on our fears, we will draw in more fear. You are setting the direction of your life with your thoughts.

CONSIDER THIS: How can you tell whether a thought is from God, from within your own mind, or a destructive thought from the enemy? Easy. If it's a negative thought, it's from the enemy. If it's a discouraging, destructive thought; if it brings fear, worry, doubt, or unbelief; if the thought makes you feel weak, inadequate, or insecure, I can guarantee you that thought is not from God. You need to deal with it immediately. In the space below, write down at least one of the negative thoughts that constantly resurface in your mind. Below that, write in bold print, "THESE THOUGHTS ARE NOT FROM GOD." Now, begin a new list of positive, true thoughts, ideas, and concepts that you choose to dwell on to replace the negative ones.

_____

_____

_____

_____

_____

_____

_____

_____

_____

_____

_____

_____

Do not go where the path
may lead, go instead where
there is no path and
leave a trail.

—*Ralph Waldo Emerson*

WHAT THE SCRIPTURES SAY

Strip yourselves of your former nature [put off and discard your old unrenewed self] . . . and be constantly renewed in the spirit of your mind [having a fresh mental and spiritual attitude], and put on the new nature (the regenerate self) created in God's image, [Godlike] in true righteousness and holiness.

—*Ephesians 4:22–24 AMP*

As [a person] thinks in his heart, so is he.

—*Proverbs 23:7 NKJV*

The weapons of our warfare are not carnal but mighty in God for pulling down strongholds, casting down arguments and every high thing that exalts itself against the knowledge of God, bringing every thought captive to the obedience of Christ.

—*2 Corinthians 10:4–5 NKJV*

A PRAYER FOR TODAY

Father, I'm excited about today. This is a day You have made; I'm going to rejoice and be glad in it. God, I know You reward those who seek You, so I thank You in advance for Your blessings, favor, and victory in my life. Thank You for ensuring my success. Thank You that I am blessed, and I cannot be cursed.

_____

_____

_____

_____

_____

_____

_____

_____

Change your thoughts and
you change your world.

—*Norman Vincent Peale*

TAKEAWAY TRUTH: Today, I will make the choice to keep my mind focused on higher things. It's not going to happen automatically. I must be determined and put forth some effort if I'm going to set my mind on the good things of God.

DAY 2:

GOD BELIEVES IN YOU

KEY TRUTH: There is no such thing as the wrong side of the tracks with our God.

If you can catch a glimpse of how much confidence God has in you, you will never again shrink back into an inferiority complex. You will rise up with boldness. When we know that somebody we respect has confidence in us, it often inspires us to believe better of ourselves. More often than not, we'll rise to the occasion and meet that person's expectations.

The enemy in your mind says that you don't have what it takes. God says you do have what it takes. Whom are you going to believe? The enemy says you're not able to succeed. God says you can do all things through Christ. The enemy says you'll never get out of debt. God says not only are you going to get out of debt, you will lend and not borrow. The enemy says you're never going to get well. God says He is restoring health unto you. The enemy says you'll never amount to anything. God says He is going to raise you up and make your life significant. The enemy says your problems are too big, there's no hope. God says He is going to solve those problems; moreover, He is going to turn them around and use them for your good.

CONSIDER THIS: Friend, start believing what God says about you, and start thinking God's thoughts. God's thoughts will fill you with faith and hope and victory. God's thoughts will build you up and encourage you. They will give you the strength you need to keep on keeping on. God's thoughts will give you that can-do mentality. Read the Scripture passages in this section and meditate on them. Then respond to these truths in the space below.

If you think about disaster, you will get it. Brood about death and you hasten your demise. Think positively and masterfully, with confidence and faith, and life becomes more secure, more fraught with action, richer in achievement and experience.

—*Eddie Rickenbacker*

_____

_____

_____

_____

_____

_____

_____

_____

_____

WHAT THE SCRIPTURES SAY

Set your minds on things above, not on earthly things.

—*Colossians 3:2* NIV

Summing it all up, friends, I'd say you'll do best by filling your minds and meditating on things true, noble, reputable, authentic, compelling, gracious—the best, not the worst; the beautiful, not the ugly; things to praise, not things to curse. Put into practice what you learned from me, what you heard and saw and realized. Do that, and God, who makes everything work together, will work you into his most excellent harmonies.

—*Philippians 4:8–9* THE MESSAGE

A PRAYER FOR TODAY

Lord, I'm eternally grateful that You love me just as I am. When I start to believe what the world says about who I am, when I begin to allow the negative thoughts of the enemy to invade my mind, please remind me that You don't believe those lies. You believe in me. It doesn't matter to You whether my family tree isn't that impressive or whether I'm successful by society's standards. You think I'm amazing! Increase my faith to see myself as You see me, to believe the truth You've spoken over my life and to live expecting Your best for me.

_____

Cast all your cares on God;
that anchor holds.

—*Alfred, Lord Tennyson*

TAKEAWAY TRUTH: Now that I understand how much God believes in me, nothing can stop me from fulfilling my destiny.

DAY 3:

IT'S ALL IN THE PROGRAMMING

KEY TRUTH: God made you, and He programmed you for victory.

YOUR MIND IS SIMILAR TO A COMPUTER. WHAT YOU PROGRAM into it determines how it will function. Think about it: You can have the most powerful computer in the world, but if you program it with the wrong software, or misinformation, it will never function as the manufacturer intended.

Beyond that, we now have a myriad of computer viruses existent in cyberspace, just lurking, looking for an opportunity to destroy your hard drive and the information stored in your computer. Such viruses can get into a perfectly good computer and start to contaminate the software. Before long the computer will develop a sluggishness; it will malfunction. Usually these problems occur not because the computer is defective, but because somebody has reprogrammed the software, or contaminated good, valuable programs or information within.

You were created in the image of God. Before you were ever formed, He programmed you to live an abundant life, to be happy, healthy, and whole. But too often we allow negative thoughts, words, and other devious viruses to access our minds, subtly changing our "software," or corrupting our information and values. When that happens, our thinking becomes impaired because it is not in line with God's Word. We make serious mistakes and wrong choices. We go through life with low self-esteem, worries, fears, feelings of inadequacy and insecurity. Making matters worse, we then pass on our negative attitudes to others.

When you recognize these things happening, you must reprogram your computer. You must change your thinking. Understand, *you* are not defective. God made you, and He has programmed you for victory. But until you get your thinking in line with your owner's manual, God's Word, you will never operate to your full potential.

CONSIDER THIS: When we're always worried, upset, or depressed, all we're really doing is delaying God in bringing the victory. God works where there's an attitude of faith. Jesus said, "If you believe, all things are possible," and the opposite of that is true as well. If you are going through a tough time in your life, even if you don't feel like keeping a positive attitude—which, at times, you probably won't—make a conscious effort to do it anyway, knowing that every minute you allow yourself to lapse into a negative attitude is a minute God cannot work in that situation. What seemingly impossible situation in your life will you determine to give over to God today, confident in His ability to bring the victory? Write about that situation in the space below.

_____

_____

_____

_____

_____

_____

_____

_____

_____

_____

_____

_____

_____

—————⧜—————

Every evening I turn my
worries over to God. He's
going to be up all night
anyway.

—*Mary C. Crowley*

WHAT THE SCRIPTURES SAY

You will keep in perfect peace him whose mind is steadfast, because he trusts in you.

—*Isaiah 26:3* NIV

Consider Him who has endured such hostility by sinners against
Himself, so that you will not grow weary and lose heart.

—*Hebrews 12:3* NASB

This is what the LORD says to you: "Do not be afraid or discouraged because of this vast army. For the battle is not yours,
but God's."

—*2 Chronicles 20:15* NIV

A PRAYER FOR TODAY

Father, today, help me to remain in an attitude of faith,
knowing that You are preparing the way for me. I may not see
anything happening with my natural eyes, but I won't let that

discourage me, because I believe You are at work. You are already bringing the victory over the difficult situations in my life. Thank You, God.

_____

_____

_____

_____

_____

_____

_____

_____

What we are is God's gift to
us. What we become is our
gift to God.

—*Eleanor Powell*

TAKEAWAY TRUTH: I refuse to go backward in my faith. I am going forward with God. I will stay focused and full of hope, knowing that God is fighting my battles for me. I'm going to be the person He wants me to be.

DAY 4:

THE MIRACLE IN YOUR MOUTH

KEY TRUTH: What you say in the midst of your difficulties will have a great impact on how long you stay in those situations.

JOSÉ LIMA STARRED AS A PITCHER WITH THE HOUSTON ASTROS for several years in the late 1990s. José is an outgoing, energetic, likable young ballplayer who usually exudes a positive attitude. But when the Astros built their new ballpark, known now as Minute Maid Park, José was upset. The fence in left field was much closer than the fence at the Astrodome. In fact, Minute Maid Park has one of the shortest distances from home plate to the left-field fence of any ballpark in Major League Baseball. The hitters love it, but the short left field makes it tougher on the pitchers, especially when they are working against right-handed batters who tend to hit to left field.

The first time José Lima stepped onto the new diamond, he walked out to the pitcher's mound, and when he looked into the outfield, he immediately noticed the close proximity of that left-field fence. "I'll never be able to pitch in here," he said.

The next season, despite the enthusiasm of the fans and the excitement of playing in that brand-new ballpark, José had the worst year of his career. He plummeted from being a twenty-game winner to being a sixteen-game loser in back-to-back seasons. Never in the history of the Astros franchise had any pitcher experienced such a pronounced negative turnaround.

What happened to José? The same thing that happens to many of us every day—we get what we say. Our words have tremendous power, and whether we want to or not, we will give life to what we're saying, either good or bad.

CONSIDER THIS: The Bible clearly tells us to speak to our mountains. Maybe your mountain is a sickness; perhaps your mountain is a troubled relationship; maybe your mountain is a floundering business. Whatever your mountain is, you must do more than think about it, more than pray about it; you must speak to that obstacle. The Bible says, "Let the weak say I'm strong. Let the oppressed say I'm free. Let the sick say I'm healed. Let the poor say I'm well off." (See Joel 3:10, Luke 4:18, Isaiah 40:29, Psalm 22:26.)

Stop talking to God about how big your mountains are, and start talking to your mountains about how big your God is! In the space below, begin speaking to your mountains.

_____

_____

_____

_____

_____

_____

_____

_____

_____

_____

_____

—————⊰⊱—————

_____

People see God every day,
_____
they just don't recognize him.

_____   —*Pearl Bailey*

_____   ▄▄▄▄▄▄▄▄▄▄▄▄▄▄

_____

_____

_____

WHAT THE SCRIPTURES SAY

The tongue is a small part of the body, but it makes great boasts.

—*James 3:4* NIV

"Have faith in God," Jesus answered . . . "Whatever you ask for
in prayer, believe that you have received it, and it will be yours."

—*Mark 11:22–24* NIV

A PRAYER FOR TODAY

Father, I'm tired of all the nagging, complaining, whining,
and wondering. I'm tired of all the fear and worry and feelings
of unworthiness and misery. Forgive me for my weak, anemic
faith, and help me get rid of all that negative talk and those discouraging thoughts. Renew my mind, enabling me to speak
words of blessing and healing over my life and the lives of

others. Remind me of Your power each day, and in Your grace allow those words of blessing to come to fruition.

_____

_____

_____

_____

_____

_____&_____

Every happening, great and small, is a parable whereby God speaks to us, and the art of life is to get the message.

—*Malcolm Muggeridge*

TAKEAWAY TRUTH: I am valuable. I am loved. God has a great plan for my life. I have favor wherever I go. God's blessings are chasing me down and overtaking me. With that in mind, I can dare to speak positively about every situation I face.

DAY 5:

GOD IS LISTENING FOR HIS WORD

KEY TRUTH: Avoiding negative words is not enough. You must be on the offensive.

IN 1981, MY MOTHER WAS DIAGNOSED WITH CANCER AND given just a few weeks to live. Medical science had reached the limits of what it could do. The best and brightest doctors in the world had exhausted their efforts, so they basically sent our mom home to die.

But we serve a supernatural God. He is not limited to the laws of nature. He can do what human beings cannot do. He can make a way in your life where it looks as if there is no way. That's what we prayed that He would do in Mother's life.

And my mother never gave up. She didn't complain about how sick or weak she felt or how hopeless her situation looked. No, she started speaking faith-filled words. She started calling in health and calling in healing. All during the day, we'd hear her going through the house speaking aloud, "I will live and not die, and I will declare the works of the Lord." She was like a walking Bible!

Mother mixed her words with God's words, and something powerful began to happen. Her circumstances began to change. Not overnight, but little by little, she began to feel better. She got her appetite back and started gaining weight. Slowly but surely, she got her strength back.

What was happening? God was watching over His word to perform it.

CONSIDER THIS: Just as it is imperative that we see ourselves as God sees us and regard ourselves as God regards us, it is equally important that we say about ourselves what God says about us. Our words are vital in bringing our dreams to pass. It's not enough to simply see your dream by faith or in your imagination. You have to begin speaking words of faith over your life. Your words have enormous creative power. The moment you speak something out, you give birth to it. This is a spiritual principle, and it works whether what you are saying is good or bad, positive or negative.

God has given us hundreds of promises, not simply for us to read and enjoy but so we might boldly declare them to bring us victory, health, hope, and abundant life. In the space below, begin to speak (write) God's Word, mixing it with your own words to confirm the Bible's truth in your own life.

_____

_____

_____

_____

_____

_____

God cannot give us happiness
and peace apart from himself,
because it is not there. There
is no such thing.

—C. S. Lewis

WHAT THE SCRIPTURES SAY

It's the word of faith that welcomes God to go to work and set things right for us. This is the core of our preaching. Say the welcoming word to God—"Jesus is my Master"—embracing, body and soul, God's work of doing in us what he did in raising Jesus from the dead. That's it. You're not "doing" anything; you're simply calling out to God, trusting him to do it for you. That's salvation. With your whole being you embrace God setting things right, and then you say it, right out loud: "God has set everything right between him and me!"

—Romans 10:8–10 THE MESSAGE

We wait in hope for the LORD; he is our help and our shield.

—Psalm 33:20 NIV

A PRAYER FOR TODAY

Father, I thank You that I am strong in the Lord and the power of Your might. I am well able to do what You have called me to do. You have called me to _____ , and today I will _____ . You have promised to be with me, to strengthen me, to cause me to succeed, and I will boldly walk in the power of Your truth, speaking Your Word into my situations.

_____

_____

_____

_____

_____

Action springs not from thought, but from a readiness for responsibility.

—*Dietrich Bonhoeffer*

_____

_____

_____

_____

_____

_____

_____

_____

_____

_____

TAKEAWAY TRUTH: When I boldly declare the promises that God made to me in His Word, when I dare to believe them and claim them as mine, all of heaven comes to attention to back up God's Word.

DAY 6:

A LEGACY OF BLESSING

KEY TRUTH: Our words affect our children's future, for either good or evil.

As parents, we can profoundly influence the direction of our children's lives by the words we say to them. I believe as husbands and wives, we can set the direction for our entire family. As a business owner, you can help set the direction for your employees. With our words, we have the ability to help mold and shape the future of anyone over whom we have influence.

And each of us has influence over somebody. You may not consider yourself a leader, but you have a sphere of influence nonetheless; somebody or some group that looks up to you. Even if you're a teenager, you have somebody who values your opinion. It is vital that we speak "good things" into our children's lives. That doesn't mean we will never disagree with them, or that we will not have to confront and correct them. But the general tenor of our conversations with our children, our words to them and our words about them, should be positive blessings.

A well-meaning mother was constantly nagging her teenage son. "You're so lazy; you're never going to amount to anything! If you don't shape up, you're never going to get into college. You'll probably wind up getting in trouble."

Those kinds of negative words will destroy a person quicker than you can imagine. You cannot speak negatively about someone on one hand, then turn around and expect that person to be blessed. If you want your son or daughter to be productive and successful, then you need to begin declaring words of life over your children, rather than predictions of doom and despair. The Scripture reminds us that with our words we can bless people or we can curse them. Today, make a choice to bless those around you with your words.

CONSIDER THIS: What are you passing down to the next generation? It's not enough to think it; you must vocalize it. A blessing is not a blessing until it is spoken. Your children (and all the children in your life) need to hear you say words such as, "I love you. I believe in you. I think you're great. There's nobody else like you. You are one of a kind." They need to hear your approval. They need to feel your love. They need your blessing. And even if your children are grown, it's never too late to begin.

Think back to your own childhood. Were there words of acceptance and approval in your life or negative, discouraging words? How did those words shape you into the person you are today?

_____

_____

_____

_____

_____

_____

_____

_____

_____

————————⚬————————

_____

_____   Words are, of course, the
                                  most powerful drug used
_____   by mankind.

_____   *—Rudyard Kipling*

_____

_____

_____

_____

WHAT THE SCRIPTURES SAY

A word aptly spoken is like apples of gold in settings of silver.

—Proverbs 25:11 NIV

Out of the same mouth proceed blessing and cursing. My brethren, these things ought not to be so.

—James 3:10 NKJV

A PRAYER FOR TODAY

Heavenly Father, help me to use the powerful tool of speech to offer words of kindness and blessing to my spouse, to my children, to my parents, to my friends, to coworkers, and even to strangers I meet throughout the day. There are so many hurting, broken people in the world who have never so much as heard a word of blessing spoken in their lives. I ask that You let me be the one to speak that word, to declare Your blessing and goodness and favor.

Syllables govern the world.

—*John Selden*

TAKEAWAY TRUTH: I will leave a legacy of blessing. I will begin today.

DAY 7:

DARE TO DECLARE

KEY TRUTH: A blessing is not a blessing until it is spoken.

YOU MUST START DECLARING GOD'S GOODNESS IN YOUR LIFE. Start boldly declaring, "God's face is smiling toward me, and He longs to be good to me." That is not bragging. That is how God says we're going to be blessed—when we start declaring His goodness.

Allow me to make some declarations in your life:

- I declare that you are blessed with God's supernatural wisdom, and you have clear direction for your life.
- I declare that you are blessed with creativity, with courage, with ability, and with abundance.
- I declare that you are blessed with a strong will and with self-control and self-discipline.
- I declare that you are blessed with a great family, with good friends, with good health, and with faith, favor, and fulfillment.

- I declare that you are blessed with success, with supernatural strength, with promotion, and with divine protection.
- I declare that you are blessed with an obedient heart and with a positive outlook on life.
- I declare that any curse ever spoken over you, any negative evil word that has ever come against you, is broken right now.
- I declare that you are blessed in the city. You are blessed in the country. You are blessed when you go in. You are blessed when you come out.
- I declare that everything you put your hands to do is going to prosper and succeed.
- I declare that you are blessed!

I encourage you to receive these words, meditate on them, let them settle deeply into your heart and mind, and become a reality in your life.

CONSIDER THIS: Remember, if you'll do your part and start boldly speaking blessings over your life and the lives of those around you, God will provide everything you need to live the life of abundance He wants you to have.

In the space below, practice writing similar blessings over your own family, your friends, and your future. If you get stumped, take one of the above blessings and appoint it to a specific person (including yourself). Then read your blessing aloud.

For example, "I declare that any negative or evil word spoken over my friend _____ is broken right now."

_____

_____

It is always wise to stop wishing for things long enough to enjoy the fragrance of those now flowering.

—*Patrice Gifford*

WHAT THE SCRIPTURES SAY

The LORD is my light and my salvation; whom shall I fear? The LORD is the strength of my life; of whom shall I be afraid?
—*Psalm 27:1 NKJV*

It is with your heart that you believe and are justified, and it is with your mouth that you confess and are saved. As the Scripture says, "Anyone who trusts in him will never be put to shame."
—*Romans 10:10–11 NIV*

A PRAYER FOR TODAY

Father, I declare Your favor and Your goodness in my life, as You've instructed me to do. Help me to be the kind of person who leaves a legacy of blessing in the lives of everyone I meet today.

We should certainly count our blessings, but we should also make our blessings count.

—*Neil A. Maxwell*

TAKEAWAY TRUTH: When I declare God's goodness in my life and in the lives of those around me, I affirm my trust in Him to accomplish His word.

STEP FOUR:

Let Go of the Past

DAY 1:

CHANGE THE CHANNEL

KEY TRUTH: Take what God has given you and make the most of it.

WE LIVE IN A SOCIETY THAT LOVES TO MAKE EXCUSES, AND ONE of our favorite phrases is "It's not my fault." But the truth is, if we are bitter and resentful, it's because we are allowing ourselves to remain that way. We've all had negative things happen to us. If you look hard enough, you can easily find reasons to have a chip on your shoulder. Anyone can make excuses and blame the past for his or her bad attitude, poor choices, or hot temper.

You may have valid reasons. Perhaps you've gone through things that nobody deserves to experience in life—physical, verbal, sexual, or emotional abuse. Maybe you've struggled to deal with a chronic illness or some other irreparable physical problem. Perhaps somebody took advantage of you in business and you lost your shirt, as well as your self-esteem. Those all are horrible experiences that no one should have to endure, but if you want to live in victory, you cannot use past emotional wounds as an excuse for making poor choices today.

You have to learn to let go of the past, to let go of your excuses (and even valid reasons), and stop feeling sorry for yourself. It's time to get rid of your victim mentality. Quit comparing your life to someone else's, and quit dwelling on what could have been, should have been, or might have been. Quit asking questions such as "Why this?" or "Why that?" or "Why me?"

You can't do anything about what's happened to you, but you can choose how you will face what's in front of you. Don't hold on to feelings of bitterness and resentment and let them poison your future. Let go of those hurts and pains. Forgive the people who did you wrong. Forgive yourself for the mistakes you may have made.

CONSIDER THIS: We all know how to use the remote control to change the channels on the TV. If we see something we don't like, no big deal—we just flip channels. We need to learn how to mentally change channels when negative images of the past pop up in our minds unexpectedly.

In the space below, create a new TV channel for your mind. Perhaps "Today's Success" channel (TSTV), where you envision enjoying the completion of a project that was a long time in coming. Now program this channel with positive memories to replace the ones you're leaving behind. Be sure to delete the "Past Failures" (PFTV) channel and the "Broken Heart" (BHTV) channels.

_____

_____

_____

_____

_____

_____

_____

_____

_____

_____   ━━━━━❦━━━━━

_____   When one door closes
_____   another door opens; but we
_____   so often look so long and so
_____   regretfully upon the closed
_____   door, that we do not see the
_____   ones which open for us.

_____   —*Alexander Graham Bell*

_____   ━━━━━━━━━━━━

_____

_____

_____

_____

WHAT THE SCRIPTURES SAY

When Jesus saw him lying there and learned that he had been in this condition for a long time, he asked him, "Do you want to get well?"

—John 5:6 NIV

Come to me, all you who are weary and burdened, and I will give you rest.

—Matthew 11:28 NIV

A PRAYER FOR TODAY

Dear Father, forgive me if I've blamed You for the heartaches and losses in my life. Forgive me for the times I've been angry when things didn't seem fair. I know now that I will never be truly happy as long as I harbor bitterness in my heart. I'm tired of feeling sorry for myself. Please help me to let go of the anger and bitterness that have sprung up in my life, and work the soil of my heart so those seeds cannot begin to grow again. Thank You, Lord, for Your mercy and for refocusing my heart and mind on Your goodness in my life.

There are no hopeless situations; there are only people who have grown hopeless about them.

—*Clare Boothe Luce*

TAKEAWAY TRUTH: Today, I'm grabbing the remote control in my mind and changing the channel. I will no longer focus on the pain or failure in my past, but on the bright and beautiful future I have with God beginning today.

DAY 2:

———— ❧ ————

GET UP AND GET MOVIN'

KEY TRUTH: To stop living in the past, to be healthy in mind, body, and spirit, you must get up and move toward your future.

IN THE BIBLE, WE READ ABOUT A MAN IN JERUSALEM WHO HAD been crippled for thirty-eight years. He spent every day of his life lying on a mat by the pool of Bethesda, hoping for a miracle. This man had a deep-seated, lingering disorder.

Many people today have lingering disorders. Their maladies may not be physical; they may be emotional, but they are deep-seated, lingering disorders nonetheless. Like the story in John 5 about the invalid lying by the pool of Bethesda, some people sit back year after year, waiting for a miracle to happen, waiting for some big event to come along to make everything better.

One day Jesus saw the man lying there in need. It was obvious that he was crippled, but Jesus asked a simple, straightforward question: "Do you want to get well?" The man's response was interesting. He began listing all of his excuses. "I'm all alone. I don't have anyone to help me. Other people have let me down. Other people always seem to get ahead of me. I don't have a chance in life." Is it any wonder he was in that condition for thirty-eight years?

Jesus didn't even respond to his sad story. He didn't say, "Yes, friend, I agree with you. You've had a tough time. Let me commiserate with you."

No, Jesus looked at him and said in effect, "If you are serious about getting well, if you are serious about getting your life in order, if you really want to get out of this mess, here's what you must do: Get up off the ground, take up your bed, and be on your way." When the man did what Jesus told him, he was miraculously healed!

CONSIDER THIS: If you're serious about being well, if you really want to be made physically and emotionally whole, you must get up and get moving with your life. No more lying around feeling sorry for yourself. Stop making excuses; stop blaming circumstances or people who disappointed you. Instead, start forgiving the people who hurt you.

Make a list of the people in your life from whom you need forgiveness or to whom you need to extend forgiveness. Briefly describe the situation related to each person. Then when you're finished, pray the prayer below over this list.

_____

_____

_____

_____

_____

_____

_____

Do we not see God at work in our circumstances? Dark times are allowed and come to us through the sovereignty of God. Are we prepared to let God do what He wants with us? . . . God is never in a hurry. If we are willing to wait, we will see God pointing out that we have been interested only in His blessings, instead of God Himself.

—*Oswald Chambers*

WHAT THE SCRIPTURES SAY

Do not judge, and you will not be judged. Do not condemn, and you will not be condemned. Forgive, and you will be forgiven.

—*Luke 6:37 NIV*

Make this your common practice: Confess your sins to each other and pray for each other so that you can live together whole and healed.

—*James 5:16 THE MESSAGE*

A PRAYER FOR TODAY

Lord, I'm answering the question You posed to the man at the pool: "Yes, I want to be well." I want to get rid of my bitterness and disappointments and begin the process of letting go of the past. Lord, I pray for the grace to forgive the people I listed in this journal, those who've hurt me. Please give me the courage to ask forgiveness from those I've wounded. Help me begin today to release any anger and resentment I've held deep in my heart, and make me emotionally whole again. Thank You, Father, for setting me free!

He who cannot forgive others, breaks the bridge over which he himself must pass.

—*Corrie ten Boom*

TAKEAWAY TRUTH: Today, I will dare to trust God. I know I cannot change the disappointment and pain of my past, so I will not try. But I will stay in an attitude of faith, believing God will use this pain to my advantage, and that the outcome will be even better than it would have been had I never been hurt.

DAY 3:

BITTERNESS BE GONE

KEY TRUTH: A bitter root will produce bitter fruit.

IF YOU WANT TO LIVE YOUR BEST LIFE NOW, YOU MUST BE QUICK to forgive. Learn to let go of the hurts and pains of the past. Don't let bitterness take root in your life. Maybe something happened to you when you were younger, someone mistreated you, someone took advantage of you. Or perhaps someone cheated you out of a promotion. Someone lied about you. Maybe a good friend betrayed you, and you have good reason to be angry and bitter.

For your emotional and spiritual health, you must let your anger and/or bitterness go. It doesn't make sense to hold on to it. After all, you can't do anything about the past, but you can do something about the future. You might as well forgive the people who offended you, and start trusting God to make it up to you.

The Scripture says, "See that . . . no root of resentment (rancor, bitterness, or hatred) shoots forth and causes trouble and bitter torment, and the many become contaminated and defiled by it" (Hebrews 12:15 AMP). Notice, bitterness is described as a root. Think about that. You can't see a root; it's deep down under the ground. But you can be sure of this: A bitter root will produce bitter fruit. If we have bitterness on the inside, it's going to affect every area of our lives.

Many people attempt to bury the hurt and pain deep in their hearts or in their subconscious minds. They don't realize it, but much of their inner turmoil is because their own heart is poisoned. The Bible says, "Keep your heart with all diligence, for out of it spring the issues of life" (Proverbs 4:23 NKJV). In other words, if we have bitterness on the inside, it's going to end up contaminating everything that comes out of us. It will contaminate our personalities and our attitudes, as well as how we treat other people.

CONSIDER THIS: In the space below, dare to go deeper. Dare to check the root of the fruit. If you're harboring anger, ask yourself why. If you have trouble getting along with other people, if you're always negative—about yourself, about others, about life in general, dare to ask yourself, "What produced this anger in me?" When you get to the root, you'll be able to deal with the problem, overcome it, and can truly begin to change.

_____

_____

_____

_____

_____

_____

_____

_____

> When you forgive, you in no
> way change the past—
> but you sure do change
> the future.
>
> —*Bernard Meltzer*

WHAT THE SCRIPTURES SAY

See to it that no one misses the grace of God and that no bitter root grows up to cause trouble and defile many.

—*Hebrews 12:15* NIV

Forgive us our sins, just as we have forgiven those who have sinned against us.

—*Matthew 6:12* NLT

A PRAYER FOR TODAY

Lord, today I pray like the psalmist David, "Search me, O God, and know my heart; test my thoughts. Point out anything you find in me that makes you sad" (Psalm 139:24 TLB). If there's even the smallest root of bitterness in me, please dig it up and remove it. If there's the smallest sign of resentment, decontaminate my heart and get rid of it. Above all, I want to please You. Reveal anything that might keep me from being free.

_____

_____

_____

_____

_____

_____

_____

If you are suffering from a bad man's injustice, forgive him, lest there be two bad men.

—*Augustine*

TAKEAWAY TRUTH: When I hold on to the poison of the past, I'm hurting only myself. But I can be made whole through forgiveness.

DAY 4:

TOXIC-FREE

KEY TRUTH: Forgiveness is the key to being free.

A FEW DECADES AGO, SEVERAL AMERICAN COMPANIES WERE authorized by the U.S. government to bury toxic waste products underground. They filled large metal containers with chemical waste, sealed the drums tightly, and buried them deep down below the topsoil. They thought that was the end of it. Within a short time, however, many of the containers began to leak and the toxic waste started seeping to the surface, causing all sorts of problems. In some locations, it killed off the vegetation and ruined the water supply. People had to move out of their homes. In one section near Niagara Falls, known as the Love Canal, an inordinate number of people began dying of cancer and other debilitating diseases. Many communities are still suffering from the effects of toxic waste burials to this day.

What went wrong? They tried to bury something that was too toxic. It couldn't be contained. They thought they could bury it and be rid of it, once and for all. But they never dreamed that the materials they were attempting to bury were so powerful. Had they disposed of them properly in the first place, they wouldn't have had the terrible problem.

It's the same with us. When someone hurts us, instead of letting it go and trusting God to make it up to us, we sometimes bury the hurt deep down on the inside. And unfortunately, just as toxic waste tends to resurface, one day the things you have tamped into your subconscious, or buried deeply in the recesses of your heart, will rise to the surface and begin to contaminate your life. We can't live with poison inside us and not expect it to eventually do us harm.

CONSIDER THIS: Face it. You are not strong enough to contain the toxicity in your life. You need help from someone bigger and stronger than yourself. That's why you need to give bitterness, resentment, and other contaminants to God. Forgiveness is the key to being free from toxic bitterness.

In the space below, explore the toxic waste that has surfaced in your life. Write out when and why you buried it. How has it impacted your life? How do you want to deal with it now?

_____

_____

_____

_____

_____

_____

_____

_____

_____

_____

_____

_____

_____

_____

_____

_____   ———————❧———————

_____

_____   Bitterness and distress are in
                                           the depth of all things. This is
_____   the groaning of the creatures,
                                           of which St. Paul speaks. But
_____   in us creation rests from its
                                           anguish, when our hearts
_____   rest in God.

_____   *—Ernesto Cardenal*

_____

_____   ————————————————

_____

_____

_____

WHAT THE SCRIPTURES SAY

Get rid of all bitterness, rage and anger, brawling and slander, along with every form of malice. Be kind and compassionate to one another, forgiving each other, just as in Christ God forgave you.

—Ephesians 4:31–32 NIV

The LORD is good to all, and His tender mercies are over all his works.

—Psalm 145:9 NKJV

A PRAYER FOR TODAY

Father, I am not strong enough to contain the toxicity in my life. I'm hardheaded and stubborn, and I don't let go easily. I need You to help me. Release me from the bitterness, resentment, and other contaminants that have leaked into my life after years of being buried beneath the surface.

I will not permit any man to narrow and degrade my soul by making me hate him.

—*Booker T. Washington*

TAKEAWAY TRUTH: Forgiveness is the key to being free. Today, I will ask for forgiveness and give it freely, without being asked.

DAY 5:

FREE TO BE YOU

KEY TRUTH: Forgiveness is a choice, but not an option.

A SHIP WAS SAILING ON A NIGHT OF PITCH-BLACK DARKNESS. Suddenly, the captain noticed a bright light directly in front of him, and he knew that his ship was on a collision course with the light. He rushed to the radio and sent an urgent message, demanding that the vessel change its course ten degrees east.

A few seconds later, he received a message in return: "Cannot do it. Change your course ten degrees west."

The captain got angry. He sent another cryptic message: "I'm a navy captain. I demand you change your course."

He received a message back a few seconds later: "I'm a seaman second class. Cannot do it. Change your course."

The captain was now furious. He sent one final message: "I'm a battleship, and I'm not changing my course!"

He got a curt message in return: "I'm a lighthouse. It's your choice, sir."

Many times we are like that navy captain; we can be hardheaded and stubborn. We can think of all the reasons why we're not going to change. *They have hurt me too badly. They did me too much wrong. I'm not going to forgive.*

No, you must change your course. The lighthouse cannot move. It must be you who moves. When you hold on to unforgiveness, you are headed for trouble. You are on a destructive path. God is saying, Change your course.

CONSIDER THIS: If you want to be happy, if you want to be free, you must be willing to change your course when God shows you a better way. Search your heart. When God brings issues to light, be quick to deal with them. If you'll do your part to begin the cleanup, you'll see God's favor and blessing in a new way. Describe some areas in which you would like to see some course changes in your life. How will you begin?

As it turns out, we do not have a little, tame, domestic God, thank God, but we do have a huge, wild, dangerous God—dangerous of course only if we think that God ought to be manageable and safe; a God of almost manic creativity, ingenuity, and enthusiasm; a Big-Enough God, who is also a supremely generous and patient God; a God of beauty and chance and solidarity.

—*Sara Maitland*

WHAT THE SCRIPTURES SAY

If you forgive men when they sin against you, your heavenly Father will also forgive you. But if you do not forgive men their sins, your Father will not forgive your sins.

—*Matthew 6:14–15* NIV

If it is possible, as much as depends on you, live peaceably with all men.

—*Romans 12:18* NKJV

A PRAYER FOR TODAY

Father, I'm believing Your Word today, expecting to receive your blessing and favor in my life. I am determined to break down any walls between us, and I ask Your help in the demolition. I want nothing but open, honest communication between You and me, and I'm ready to let go of the wrongs that have been done to me. I'm willing to do what it takes to experience a freshness in my relationship with You and with others.

Be not angry that you cannot make others as you wish them to be, since you cannot make yourself as you wish to be.

—*Thomas à Kempis*

TAKEAWAY TRUTH: The lighthouse is not moving. I must change my course.

DAY 6:

THE GOD OF PAYBACK

KEY TRUTH: Trust God to bring about the justice in your life.

GOD HAS PROMISED IF WE WILL PUT OUR TRUST IN HIM, HE will pay us back for all the unfair things that have happened to us (see Isaiah 61:7–9). Maybe you were cheated in a business deal and you lost a lot of money. Maybe somebody lied about you, and that misinformation kept you from getting a promotion. Or maybe a good friend betrayed you.

Certainly, these kinds of losses leave indelible scars, causing you to want to hold on to your grief. It would be logical for you to seek revenge. Many people would even encourage you to do so. The slogan "Don't get mad, get even!" is a commonly accepted principle in America today.

But that is not God's plan for you. If you want to live your best life now, you must learn to trust God to bring about the justice in your life. The Bible says that God is a just God, and He will settle and solve the cases of His people (see Deuteronomy 32:4 NLT; Hebrews 10:30 AMP). That means you don't have to go around trying to pay everybody back for the wrong things they've done to you. You don't have to go around trying to get even with people. God is your vindicator. Let Him fight your battles for you. Let God settle your cases. God has promised if you'll turn matters over to Him and let Him handle them His way, He'll make your wrongs right. He'll bring justice into your life.

CONSIDER THIS: When you know that God is fighting your battles, you can walk with a new confidence, with a spring in your step, a smile on your face, and a song in your heart. You are free! When you truly understand that you don't have to fix everything that happens to you, you don't have to get all upset and try to pay somebody back for what they did or didn't do, you don't have to worry, you don't have to try to manipulate the situation or control the circumstances or people involved.

When you have this kind of attitude, you are leaving the door wide open for God to pay you back. And remember, God always pays back abundantly. In the space below, respond to what you've just read, sharing the battles you're leaving in God's hands.

_____

_____

_____

_____   ⸙

_____
                                 Bitterness imprisons life; love
_____   releases it.

_____   —*Henry Emerson Fosdick*

_____   ━━━━━━━━━━━━━━━

_____

_____

_____

_____

_____

_____

_____

WHAT THE SCRIPTURES SAY

Never avenge yourselves, but leave the way open for [God's] wrath.

—*Romans 12:19* AMP

Let us not grow weary while doing good, for in due season we shall reap if we do not lose heart.

—*Galatians 6:9* NKJV

A PRAYER FOR TODAY

Lord, I pray for the wisdom to leave all my battles in Your hands. I believe You are working, even now, to settle the frustrating or hurtful situations in my life. You promised to take any evil that comes against me and turn it around for my advantage. I claim that promise, and I know You're going to make this up to me. I know You will prosper me wherever I go, and You will bring about justice in my life.

To let go is surrender; to let God is belief.

—*A. W. Tozer*

TAKEAWAY TRUTH: God sees every wrong that has been done to me. He's taking notes and keeping a record, so I don't have to.

DAY 7:

BYGONES BE GONE

KEY TRUTH: Never put a question mark where God has put a period.

ONE OF THE MOST IMPORTANT KEYS TO LIVING YOUR BEST LIFE now, as well as to moving forward into the great future God has for you, is learning how to overcome the disappointments in life. Because disappointments can pose such formidable obstacles to letting go of the past, you need to be sure you have dealt with this area before taking the next step to living at your full potential.

Often, defeating disappointments and letting go of the past are the flip sides of the same coin, especially when you are disappointed in yourself. When you do something wrong, don't hold on to it and beat yourself up about it. Admit it, seek forgiveness, and move on. Be quick to let go of your mistakes and failures, hurts, pains, and sins.

The disappointments that disturb us the most, however, are usually those caused by other people. Many individuals who have been hurt by others are missing out on their new beginnings because they keep reopening old wounds. But no matter what we have gone through, no matter how unfair the situation was or how disappointed we were, we must release the hurt and let it go.

God wants to do more than you can ask or think. He wants to restore good things to you in abundance. If you will focus on the right things, God will take your most horrendous battlefield and turn it into your greatest blessing field.

CONSIDER THIS: You may have made some poor choices that have caused you awful heartache and pain. Perhaps you feel that you have blown it, that your life is in shambles, beyond repair. You may feel disqualified from God's best, convinced that you must settle for second best the rest of your life because of the poor decisions you made. But friend, God desires your restoration even more than you do! If you'll let go of the past and start living each day with faith and expectancy, God will restore everything the enemy has stolen from you.

Talk to God in the space below about the disappointments or mistakes in your past that have kept you from moving forward. Declare that you are willing to begin letting go.

_____

_____

_____

_____

_____

_____

_____

_____

_____

_____

_____

_____   ❧

_____   Courage is fear that has said
                                              its prayers.
_____
                                        —*Dorothy Bernard*
_____

_____

_____

_____

_____

WHAT THE SCRIPTURES SAY

Forgetting what is behind and straining toward what is ahead, I
press on toward the goal.

—*Philippians 3:13* NIV

The LORD is wonderfully good to those who wait for him and
seek him.

—*Lamentations 3:25* NLT

A PRAYER FOR TODAY

Lord, I ask You for the courage and determination to shake
off the disappointments of the past. Please take my scars and

turn them into stars for Your glory. Let my life be a testimony to what Your grace can do. I'm pressing on. I'm moving forward, knowing that You have great things in store for me.

_____

_____

_____

_____

_____

Do not let what you cannot do interfere with what you can do.

—*John Wooden*

_____

_____

_____

_____

_____

_____

_____

_____

TAKEAWAY TRUTH: I can't unscramble eggs. What's done is done. I must move forward.

Step Five:

Find Strength
Through Adversity

DAY 1:

STANDING FIRM

KEY TRUTH: Even when we are sitting down on the outside, we must see ourselves standing on the inside!

WE ALL FACE CHALLENGES IN LIFE. WE ALL HAVE THINGS THAT come against us. We may get knocked down on the outside, but the key to living in victory is to learn how to get up on the inside.

I heard a story about a little boy who was in church with his mother, and he had so much energy, he just could not sit still. In fact, he kept standing up on the seat. His mother said, "Son, sit down."

He'd sit down for a few seconds, then he'd get right back up again.

She'd gently reprimand him again, "Son, I said to sit down!"

This happened several times, and then the little boy stood up and simply would not sit down. His mother took her hand, put it on his head, and pushed him down onto the seat. The boy sat there smiling. Finally, he looked at his mother and said, "Mom,

I may be sitting down on the outside, but I'm standing up on the inside!"

CONSIDER THIS: No matter what you are going through or how difficult it may seem, you can remain standing on the inside. It may take courage; it will definitely take determination, but you can do it if you decide to do so. You must act on your will, not simply your emotions.

You may be sitting around waiting for God to change your circumstances. *Then* you're going to be happy, *then* you're going to have a good attitude, *then* you're going to give God praise. But God is waiting on you to get up on the inside. When you do your part, He'll begin to change things, then He'll work supernaturally in your life.

In what ways have you been allowing adversity to impact your joy? Your passion? Your life?

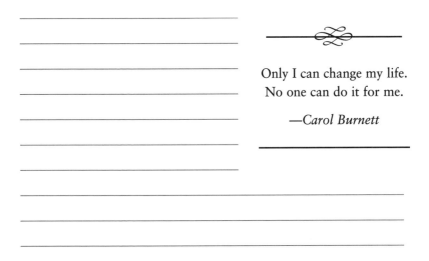

Only I can change my life.
No one can do it for me.

—*Carol Burnett*

WHAT THE SCRIPTURES SAY

Use every piece of God's armor to resist the enemy in the time of evil, so that after the battle you will still be standing firm.

—*Ephesians 6:13* NLT

Be strong. Take heart. Payday is coming!

—*2 Chronicles 15:7* THE MESSAGE

David encouraged and strengthened himself in the Lord His God.

—*1 Samuel 30:6* AMP

A PRAYER FOR TODAY

God, I'm determined not to let adversity defeat me. I'm getting up on the inside. No one and nothing will continue to steal my joy. Because of You and Your grace in my life, I know I'm the victor and not the victim. I'm confident that when one door closes, You're going to open a bigger and a better door. I pray for the courage to stand firm in the face of adversity, knowing You are standing with me. Thank You, Lord, for Your presence in my life.

———————————————————————

———⚮———

When you get into a tight place and everything goes against you, till it seems as though you could not hold on a minute longer, never give up then, for that is just the place and time that the tide will turn.

—*Harriet Beecher Stowe*

TAKEAWAY TRUTH: Even if people or circumstances attempt to keep me down, I will face the adversity in my life by standing courageously like the victorious overcomer God made me to be.

DAY 2:

DETERMINED TO BE HAPPY

KEY TRUTH: God has destined you to live in victory, but you have to do your part.

FRIEND, LIFE IS TOO SHORT TO TRUDGE THROUGH IT DEPRESSED and defeated. No matter what has come against you or what is causing you to slip and fall, no matter who or what is trying to push you down, you need to keep getting up on the inside. If you want to give your enemy a nervous breakdown, learn to keep a good attitude, even when the bottom falls out! Learn to be happy even when things don't go your way.

Medical science tells us that people with a determined, feisty spirit usually get well quicker than people who are prone to being negative and discouraged. That's because God made us to be determined. We were not created to live in depression and defeat. A negative spirit dries up your energy; it weakens your immune system. Many people are living with physical ailments or emotional bondage because they are not standing up on the inside.

The Bible tells us that many of the saints of old died in faith.

But you can die in faith only if you live a faith-filled life. When it's my time to go, I want to spend my last day here on this earth full of joy, full of faith, and full of victory. I've made up my mind; I'm going to live my best life now, and when my days are done, I'm going to die standing up on the inside.

When you face adversity, remind yourself, "I am full of God's can-do power. I can overcome. I can live in victory. I can stand up on the inside." Learn to tap into the can-do power that God has placed inside you, rather than rolling over in the face of adversity.

CONSIDER THIS: The great missionaries Paul and Silas were incarcerated in a prison in Philippi. Did Paul and Silas murmur and complain? Did they start blaming God or having a pity party? No, in the midst of that adversity, the Bible says, they were "praying and singing hymns of praise to God" (Acts 16:25 AMP). In other words, they were standing up on the inside. When you give God praise and stay in an attitude of faith in the midst of your adversities, God's miracle-working power will show up. The Bible records that at midnight while they were singing praises to God, suddenly there was a great earthquake. The prison doors flew open; the chains fell off Paul and Silas.

Regardless of the circumstances of your life, now is your time to praise Him. In the space below, write your own "psalm" of praise to God. It doesn't have to be perfect. Just write what's in your heart. Regardless of your circumstances, as an expression of your will, praise God for who He is, as well as what He does for you.

_____

_____

_____

Praise God even when you
don't understand what
He is doing.

—*Henry Jacobsen*

WHAT THE SCRIPTURES SAY

God, . . . renew a right, persevering, and steadfast spirit within
me.

—*Psalm 51:10* AMP

Call to me and I will answer you and tell you great and un-
searchable things you do not know.

—*Jeremiah 33:3* NIV

A PRAYER FOR TODAY

*Take the song of praise you just wrote and offer it as a prayer
to the Lord. Sing it, say it, or simply meditate on the words.
The Lord dwells in the praises of His children. Take some extra
time today to praise God for His goodness to you. (For instance, you can praise Him for your marriage partner, or the
partner He is preparing for you! You can praise Him for pro-*

viding for you physically, financially, or emotionally. In some way, allow praise to flow from your heart onto the pages of your journal.)

_____

_____

_____

_____

_____

_____

_____

_____

Only dead fish swim with
the stream.

—*Anonymous*

TAKEAWAY TRUTH: Life is a gift from God, so there's no reason to whine. No matter what happens, I am determined to live life to the fullest, knowing my happiness comes from God.

DAY 3:

ON TIME, EVERY TIME

KEY TRUTH: God often is working the most when we see and feel it the least.

HUMAN NATURE TENDS TO WANT EVERYTHING RIGHT NOW. We're always in a hurry. Most of us get impatient when we miss a turn on a revolving door! When we pray for our dreams to come to pass, we want them to be fulfilled immediately. But we have to understand, God has an appointed time to answer our prayers and to bring our dreams to pass. And the truth is, no matter how badly we want it sooner, no matter how much we pray and plead with God, it's not going to change His appointed time. It's still going to happen on God's timetable.

Because we sometimes don't understand God's timing, we live upset and frustrated, wondering when God is going to do something. "God, when are You going to change my husband? When are You going to bring me a mate? God, when is my business going to take off? When are my dreams going to come to pass?"

God is not like an ATM machine, where you punch in the

right codes and receive what you requested (assuming you've even made a deposit!). No, we all have to wait patiently. That's a part of learning to trust God. The key is, *how* are we going to wait? What will be our physical, emotional, and spiritual demeanors? Are we going to wait with a good attitude, with expectancy, knowing that God has great things in store? Or are we going to be upset, frustrated, and muttering complaints?

CONSIDER THIS: If you know you have to wait anyway, why not make a decision to enjoy your life while you're waiting? Why not be happy while God is in the process of changing things? After all, there's nothing you can really do to make it happen any faster. You might as well relax and enjoy your life, knowing that at the appointed time God is going to bring His plan to pass.

In the space below, tell God about the deepest desire of your heart and give that dream or desire to Him, trusting Him to make it come true in due season:

Keep your face to the
sunshine and you cannot see
the shadow.

—*Helen Keller*

_____

_____

_____

_____

_____

_____

_____

_____

WHAT THE SCRIPTURES SAY

I am trusting you, O LORD, saying, "You are my God!" My future is in your hands.

—*Psalm 31:14-15* NLT

The vision is yet for an appointed time . . . Though it tarry, wait [earnestly] for it, because it will surely come.

—*Habakkuk 2:3* AMP

A PRAYER FOR TODAY

God, I know You are in control of each and every day, relationship, and opportunity. You are in control of my heart's every dream and desire. Although I don't see anything happening, I believe You are working behind the scenes, and at the right time, You're going to change my life for the better. You're going to give me the desires of my heart. So, however long it takes. I'm going to wait and trust in Your plan for my life. *(In the space below, feel free to express your thoughts about the balance between frustration and patience as you await God's best.)*

To keep a lamp burning, we
have to keep putting oil in it.

—*Mother Teresa*

TAKEAWAY TRUTH: I cannot see the big picture of my
life, but God can, so I will trust His timing.

DAY 4:

THE BIG PICTURE

KEY TRUTH: Let God do it His way.

WE DON'T ALWAYS UNDERSTAND GOD'S METHODS. HIS WAYS don't always make sense to us, but we have to realize that God sees the big picture. Consider this possibility: You may be ready for what God has for you, but someone else who is going to be involved is not yet ready. God has to do a work in another person or another situation before your prayer can be answered according to God's will for your life. All the pieces have to come together to align with God's perfect timing.

But never fear; God is getting everything lined up in your life. You may not feel it; you may not see it. Your situation may look just as it did for the past ten years, but then one day, in a split second of time, God will bring it all together. When it is God's timing, all the forces of darkness can't stop Him. When it's the appointed time, no man can keep it from happening. When it's your due season, God will bring it to pass.

Suddenly, things will change. Suddenly, that business will take off. Suddenly, your husband will desire a relationship with

God. Suddenly, that wayward child will come home. Suddenly, God will bring your hopes and dreams to pass.

To live your best life now, you must learn to trust God's timing. You may not think He's working, but you can be sure, right now, behind the scenes, God is arranging all the pieces to come together to work out His plan for your life.

CONSIDER THIS: If you push hard enough, and if you're so stubborn that you must have things your way, God will sometimes allow you to undertake a project without His blessing or at the wrong time. The problem with that, of course, is when you start something in your own strength and in your own timing, you're going to have to finish it and maintain it in your own strength. The end result is a constant strain on you and a drain on your resources. Life becomes a constant struggle. Nearly all joy, peace, and victory dwindle from your existence. That is not a place of contentment and satisfaction.

On a scale of 1 to 5, with 1 being "total surrender and waiting on God," and 5 being "I'm pushing this cart myself," rate yourself on your willingness to wait on the Lord. Then reflect on how that rating impacts your life.

_____

_____

_____

_____

_____

_____

Life is a series of experiences, each one of which makes us bigger, even though it is hard to realize this. For the world was built to develop character, and we must learn that the setbacks and grieving which we endure help us in our marching onward.

—*Henry Ford*

WHAT THE SCRIPTURES SAY

Those who hope in the LORD will renew their strength. They will soar on wings like eagles; they will run and not grow weary, they will walk and not be faint.

—*Isaiah 40:31 NIV*

I waited patiently for the LORD; he turned to me and heard my cry.

—*Psalm 40:1 NIV*

A PRAYER FOR TODAY

Father, I've seen Your hand at work in my life, and I believe You have been arranging things in my favor long before I even knew. Help me to have faith, even in those circumstances that seem to be endless or unchanging. Give me joy despite my circumstances, knowing my hope is in You. Thank You, Lord, for Your perfect timing in my life.

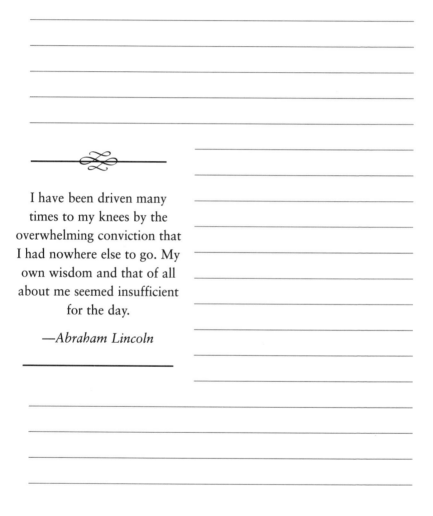

I have been driven many times to my knees by the overwhelming conviction that I had nowhere else to go. My own wisdom and that of all about me seemed insufficient for the day.

—*Abraham Lincoln*

TAKEAWAY TRUTH: When God says it's time, He will bring it to pass.

DAY 5:

FAITH THAT TESTS

KEY TRUTH: It's in the tough times of life that we find out what we're made of.

NO MATTER HOW SUCCESSFUL WE ARE, WE ALL FACE CHALLENGES, struggles, and times when things don't go our way. When calamities occur, some people immediately think they have done something wrong, that God must surely be punishing them. They don't understand that God has a divine purpose for every challenge that comes into our life. He doesn't send the problems, but sometimes He allows us to go through them.

Why is that? The Bible says temptations, trials, and difficulties must come, because if we are to strengthen our spiritual muscles and grow stronger, we must have adversities to overcome and attacks to resist. Moreover, it's in the tough times of life that we find out what we're really made of. The pressure exposes things we need to deal with—things such as wrong attitudes, wrong motives, areas where we're compromising. As odd as this may seem, the trials can be beneficial.

The Scripture says, "Do not be amazed and bewildered at the

fiery ordeal which is taking place to test your quality, as though something strange (unusual and alien to you and your position) were befalling you" (1 Peter 4:12 AMP). Notice, the trial is intended to test your quality, to test your character, to test your faith. In other words, don't think it's a big deal when you go through tough times. All through life, you will face various tests, and even though you may not enjoy them, God will use those trials to refine you. He's trying to shape you into the person He wants you to be. If you will learn to cooperate with God and be quick to change and correct the areas that He brings to light, you'll pass that test, and you will be promoted to a new level.

I've discovered that in the struggles of life, God is more interested in changing me than He is in changing my circumstances. I'm not saying that God won't change the circumstances. Certainly, He can and often does. But most of the time I'm tested in the areas where I am the weakest, so I can discover my true strength in God.

CONSIDER THIS: God is not going to change anyone we are dealing with until He first changes us. When we quit complaining about everybody around us and, instead, start taking a good look inside ourselves and working with God to change us from the inside, God will change those other people. Examine your own heart and see if there are attitudes and motives that you need to change. Write about those areas in the space below:

——————————
——————————
——————————
——————————
——————————
——————————
——————————
——————————
——————————
——————————
——————————

A successful person is one
who can lay a firm
foundation with the bricks
that others throw at
him or her.

—*David Brinkley*

WHAT THE SCRIPTURES SAY

These [trials] have come so that your faith—of greater worth
than gold, which perishes even though refined by the fire—may
be proved genuine and may result in praise, glory and honor
when Jesus Christ is revealed.

—*1 Peter 4:7* NIV

We are God's workmanship.

—*Ephesians 2:10* NIV

A PRAYER FOR TODAY

God, I am willing to change. I want to grow. I don't want to
settle for a mediocre life, and I know that's not what You created me for. So I'm going to be calm. I'm going to be patient.
Whatever circumstances happen in my life, help me to look to

You and ask what You would have me learn, how You would change me and cause me to grow. When I can do that, I know You will turn my challenges into assets, my struggles into great victories.

List below any challenges you are facing right now that are causing you to stretch and grow:

What counts is not necessarily the size of the dog in the fight—it's the size of the fight in the dog.

—*Dwight Eisenhower*

TAKEAWAY TRUTH: God is using the circumstances of my life to do a wonderful work in me.

DAY 6:

A WORK IN PROGRESS

KEY TRUTH: A trial is a test of your faith, character, and endurance.

MANY YEARS AGO, FISHING FOR CODFISH IN THE NORTHEAST had become a lucrative commercial business. The fishing industry recognized that a great market for codfish existed all over America, but they had a major problem in the distribution. At first, they simply froze the fish as they did all their other products, and shipped it out across the country. But for some reason, after the codfish was frozen, it lost its taste. So the owners decided to ship the fish in huge tanks filled with fresh seawater. They thought for sure that would solve the problem and keep the fish fresh. But to their dismay, this process only made matters worse. Because the fish were inactive in the tank, they became soft and mushy, and once again they lost their taste.

One day, somebody decided to put some catfish in the tank with the codfish. Catfish are a natural enemy of codfish, so as the tank traveled across the country, the codfish had to stay alert and active, and be on the lookout for the catfish. Amazingly, when the tank arrived at its destination, the codfish were as fresh and tasty as they were in the Northeast.

Like that catfish, perhaps adversity was dropped in your path for a purpose. It was put there to challenge you, to strengthen you, to sharpen you, to keep you fresh, to keep you alive and active and growing. Granted, at times, it feels as though you have a great white shark in the tank rather than a catfish, but the adversity you are facing could very well be something God is using to push you and challenge you to be your best. The trial is a test of your faith, character, and endurance. Don't give up. Don't quit. Don't whine and complain, saying, "God, why is all this happening to me?"

Instead, stand strong and fight the good fight of faith. God is giving you an opportunity for promotion. It is through the struggle that we find ourselves growing stronger.

CONSIDER THIS: Without opposition or resistance, there is no potential for progress. Without the resistance of air, an eagle can't soar. Without the resistance of water, a ship can't float. Without the resistance of gravity, you and I can't even walk.

In the following space, reflect on the words above and then describe other examples of resistance that makes movement possible:

_____

_____

_____

_____

_____

_____

In the middle of difficulty lies opportunity.

—*Albert Einstein*

WHAT THE SCRIPTURES SAY

Blessed (happy, to be envied) is the man who is patient under trial and stands up under temptation, for when he has stood the test and been approved, he will receive [the victor's] crown of life which God has promised to those who love Him.

—*James 1:12* AMP

We know that all things work together for good to those who love God, to those who are the called according to His purpose.

—*Romans 8:28* NKJV

Continue to work out your salvation with fear and trembling, for it is God who works in you to will and to act according to his good purpose.

—*Philippians 2:12–13* NIV

A PRAYER FOR TODAY

Thank You, Father, for the refining fire in my life; for Your loving hands that mold and remake these feet of clay into beautiful, shining testaments to your glory. Knock off my rough edges and sand down the rough spots. Soften my heart and make me more like You.

If we had no winter, the spring would not be so pleasant: if we did not sometimes taste of adversity, prosperity would not be so welcome.

—*Anne Bradstreet*

TAKEAWAY TRUTH: I will fight the good fight, working with God to deal with any issues He allows. And we will win.

DAY 7:

ONE SMALL STEP; ONE GIANT LEAP

KEY TRUTH: Adversity often pushes us into our divine destiny.

MANY PEOPLE RESPOND NEGATIVELY TO ADVERSITIES AND TROUble, rather than believing that God can bring good out of the situation. I'm not saying God sends the trouble, but I am saying God will use any adversity you face to take you to a higher level—if you'll just do your part and keep standing strong.

In my life, I've discovered two kinds of faith—a *delivering* faith and a *sustaining* faith. Delivering faith is when God instantly turns your situation around. When that happens, it's great. But I believe it takes a greater faith and a deeper walk with God to have sustaining faith. That's when circumstances don't change immediately, but you say, "God, I don't care what comes against me, I don't care how long it takes, this thing is not going to defeat me. It's not going to get me down. I know You're on my side. And as long as You are for me, that's all that matters." Sustaining faith is what gets you through those dark nights of the soul, when you don't know where to go, or what to do, and it seems that you can't last another day . . . but because of your faith in God, you do.

If you will handle adversity in the right way, God has promised that He will turn your challenges into stepping-stones for promotion. God wants to do new and unusual things in our lives. He's looking for people who will trust Him with their whole hearts. He's looking for people who won't limit Him with their small-minded thinking.

God wants you to constantly be growing, and sometimes He'll use a little adversity or some tension to get you moving forward. He will allow pressure to push you, to stretch you, to get you out of your comfort zone. He knows just how much you can take, and in your times of distress, keep in mind, God is enlarging you. The struggle is giving you strength.

CONSIDER THIS: God uses ordinary people like you and me to do extraordinary things. God is not looking for great power. He's not looking for great education. God is simply looking for a willing heart. God is not looking for ability; He's looking for availability. Just give God what you have. And He'll make more out of your life than you've ever dreamed possible.

Are you ready to step out in faith with a willing heart surrendered to God? This is an excellent time and place to tell Him so!

_____

_____

_____

_____

_____

_____

_____

_____

_____   ⤝❧⤞

_____   A pessimist sees the difficulty
                                  in every opportunity; an
_____   optimist sees the opportunity
                                  in every difficulty.
_____
                                       —*Winston Churchill*
_____

_____

_____

_____

_____

WHAT THE SCRIPTURES SAY

As the Spirit of the Lord works within us, we become more and
more like him and reflect his glory even more.

—*2 Corinthians 3:18* NLT

Is any one of you in trouble? He should pray. Is anyone happy?
Let him sing songs of praise.

—*James 5:13* NIV

A PRAYER FOR TODAY

Lord, You know the gifts and talents that You have given me.
Even when I feel as if I have none, You know better. You know
what I am capable of, even when I doubt it. I thank You that

You're doing everything necessary to move me toward my divine destiny. I am ready and willing to move beyond the safe zone and step over into the *faith* zone. Help me, Father, to not look back, but to press forward in faith.

Sweet are the thoughts that savor content; the quiet mind is richer than a crown.

—*Robert Greene*

TAKEAWAY TRUTH: God is turning my challenges into stepping-stones for my success.

STEP SIX:

Live to Give

DAY 1:

CREATED TO GIVE

KEY TRUTH: You must learn to be a giver and not a taker.

SOCIETY TEACHES US TO LOOK OUT FOR NUMBER ONE. "WHAT'S in it for me? I'll help you, but what will I get in return?" We readily acknowledge that this is a "me" generation, and that same narcissism sometimes spills over into our relationship with God, our families, and one another.

Many people nowadays are blatantly and unabashedly living for themselves. They're not interested in other people. They don't have time to help others in need. They focus only on what they want, what they need, what they feel will benefit them the most. Ironically, this selfish attitude condemns them to living shallow, unrewarding lives. No matter how much they acquire for themselves, they are never satisfied.

Friend, if you want to experience a new level of God's joy, if you want Him to pour out His blessings and favor in your life, then you're going to have to get your mind off yourself. You must learn to be a giver and not a taker. Quit trying to figure out what everybody can do for you, and start trying to figure out what you can do for somebody else. We were not made to function as self-serving people, thinking only of ourselves. No, God created us to be givers. And you will never be truly fulfilled as a human being until you learn the simple secret of how to give your life away.

You may not realize it, but it is extremely selfish to go around always dwelling on your problems, always thinking about what you want or need, but hardly noticing the many needs of others all around you. One of the best things you can do if you're having a problem is to help solve somebody else's problem. If you want your dreams to come to pass, help someone else fulfill his or her dreams. Start sowing some seeds so God can bring you a harvest. When we meet other people's needs, God meets our needs.

CONSIDER THIS: We need to look for opportunities to share God's love, His gifts, and His goodness with others. It doesn't take much to make someone happy. Money isn't required. You can share a smile. A compliment. Thanks for a service provided. Or you can do something practical: take something that is lying around your house or in storage, something you're never going to use, and offer it as a gift to someone who could use it. If it's not meeting a need, use it to sow a seed of blessing.

In the space below, answer the question "Whom can I bless today?" Write the person's name and note at least one specific way you can do just that. Now, let's get more specific. When and how will you make this specific effort to bless that person?

_____

_____

_____

_____

Don't judge each day by the
harvest you reap, but by the
seeds you plant.

—*Robert Louis Stevenson*

WHAT THE SCRIPTURES SAY

Encourage one another daily.

—*Hebrews 3:13* NIV

I want you to share your food with the hungry and to welcome
poor wanderers into your homes. Give clothes to those who
need them, and do not hide from relatives who need your help.
If you do these things, your salvation will come like the dawn.
Yes, your healing will come quickly.

—*Isaiah 58:7–8* NLT

A PRAYER FOR TODAY

Father, I thank You for the many ways You've blessed my
life. I believe You created me to encourage and bless others.
Help me to use my life—my hands, my words, my gifts, the

material things You've blessed me with—to bring healing, hope, and blessing to others. Help me take my mind off my needs and wants and focus instead on the needs of others. This is my fervent prayer.

—————————————————————

When we do the best that we can, we never know what miracle is wrought in our life, or in the life of another.

—*Helen Keller*

TAKEAWAY TRUTH: I was created to be a blessing, to give more than I receive. Today, I will look for ways to bless.

DAY 2:

BLESSED TO BLESS

KEY TRUTH: Whatever you give will be given back to you.

GIVING IS A SPIRITUAL PRINCIPLE. WHATEVER YOU GIVE WILL BE given back to you. If you give a smile, you will receive smiles from others. If you are generous to people in their time of need, God will make sure that other people are generous to you in your time of need. Interesting, isn't it? What you make happen for others, God will make happen for you.

I saw an interesting report about a young man in Saudi Arabia. He was extremely wealthy and lived in an ornate palace almost too grand to describe. He had scores of automobiles and airplanes. He owned several cruise ships just for his personal use. The man was rich beyond anything my mind could fathom.

But what intrigued me about him was the interesting way in which he used part of his wealth. Every couple of months or so, he would bring in hundreds of poor people from his country. He met with them individually and discussed their needs. Then, in most cases, he would give the people whatever they needed. If they needed a car, he would buy them a car. If they needed a home, he would buy them a home. If they needed money for an operation, he provided that, as well. Whatever the need, he would meet it. He gave away hundreds of thousands of dollars and literally millions more in property or materials. Is it any wonder why his business continues to flourish?

I doubt that the Saudi man practices the Christian faith, but the principles of giving are spiritual principles. They work regardless of nationality, skin color, or even religion. If you give unselfishly, it is going to be given back to you. If you meet other people's needs, God will make sure your own needs are supplied in abundance.

A person starts to live when he can live outside himself.

—*Albert Einstein*

CONSIDER THIS: You may be thinking, *Well, if I had all that money, I would do the same thing.* No, that's where we miss it. You have to start right where you are. You must be faithful with what you have, then God will trust you with more.

The closest thing to the heart of our God is helping hurting people. God loves when we sing and when we pray. He loves when we come together to celebrate His goodness. But nothing pleases God more than when we take care of one of His children.

In the space below, reflect on the ways God has met your needs. Write down a few specific blessings He's given you in the past year. Now pray the prayer below, praising Him for these blessings and more, and ask Him to reveal opportunities to give to others, in gratitude for all that you've been given.

You have not lived today until you have done something for someone who cannot pay you back.

—*John Bunyan*

WHAT THE SCRIPTURES SAY

I will bless you [with abundant increase of favors] and make your name famous and distinguished, and you will be a blessing [dispensing good to others].

—*Genesis 12:2* AMP

To the extent that you did it to one of these brothers of Mine, even the least of them, you did it to Me.

—*Matthew 12:40* NASB

If you help the poor, you are lending to the LORD.

—*Proverbs 19:17* NLT

A PRAYER FOR TODAY

Lord, how blessed I am to be Your child. Just in the past year, You've blessed me with _____ [*include some things you listed previously in your journal*]. You've provided for my physical needs. You've been at work in my family and in my business/work life. God, I thank You for being so kind and generous to me. Now I ask You to give me the opportunity to be a true giver—a generous, considerate, kind, and loving person who consistently seeks new ways to reach out to those in need. Please put hurting people in my path and open my eyes to see them and their needs. Free my hands, free my heart and my mind, to serve others with generosity.

_____

_____

_____

_____

_____

_____

_____

_____

TAKEAWAY TRUTH: Today, I will be on the lookout for the opportunity to give myself away. I will make a difference.

DAY 3:

LOVE IS BLIND

KEY TRUTH: God expects you to be an example of kindness and mercy.

How we treat other people can have a great impact on the degree of blessings and favor of God we are experiencing in our lives. Are you good to people? Are you kind and considerate? Do you speak and act with love in your heart and regard other people as valuable and special? Friend, you can't treat people poorly and expect to be blessed. You can't be rude and inconsiderate and expect to live in victory.

When you are placed in awkward situations where someone doesn't treat you right, you have a golden opportunity to help heal a wounded heart. Keep in mind, hurting people often hurt other people as a result of their own pain. If someone is rude and inconsiderate, you can almost be certain that they have some unresolved issues inside. They have major problems— anger, resentment, or some heartache—they are trying to cope with or overcome. The last thing they need is for you to make matters worse by responding angrily.

Evil is never overcome by more evil. If you mistreat people who are mistreating you, you will make matters worse. When you express anger to a person who has been angry with you, it's like adding fuel to a fire. No, we overcome evil with good. When someone hurts you, the only way you can overcome it is by showing them mercy, forgiving them, and doing what is right.

Keep taking the high road, being kind and courteous. Keep walking in love and having a good attitude. God sees what you're doing. He sees you going the extra mile to do what's right, and He will make sure your good actions and attitude will overcome that evil. If you'll keep doing the right thing, you will come out far ahead of where you would have been had you fought fire with fire.

CONSIDER THIS: If someone is not treating you right today, go out of your way to be kinder than usual to that person. God sees your acts of kindness and mercy. When you are kind to people, when you go around doing good to people, God arranges for others to leave "handfuls" of good things for you on purpose. You will find a handful of blessings over here, a handful of blessings over there, supernatural favors over here, unexpected promotion over there. Everywhere you go, you will discover the supernatural blessings of God lying in your path, left there on purpose for you by God.

In the space below, reflect on how you can show kindness and mercy to one who has been unkind and unmerciful to you. How can you love this person in a fresh way?

_____

_____

_____

> Treat people as if they were what they ought to be, and you help them to become what they are capable of being.
>
> —*Johann Wolfgang von Goethe*

WHAT THE SCRIPTURES SAY

The goodness of God leads you to repentance.

—*Romans 2:4 NKJV*

See that none of you repays another with evil for evil, but always aim to show kindness and seek to do good to one another and to everybody.

—*1 Thessalonians 5:15 AMP*

[Love] does not hold grudges and will hardly even notice when others do it wrong.

—*1 Corinthians 13:5 TLB*

A PRAYER FOR TODAY

God, sometimes I feel as if I'm the only one who's making any effort. In my family, at my job, I often feel that I'm getting the short end of the stick, that I'm not appreciated or loved. When I feel that way, please remind me, Father, that You see me. You keep records of every effort I make to show Your love and mercy to others. Help me not to wallow in self-pity or hold grudges against those who mistreat me, and help me to be a mirror that reflects Your love in every circumstance.

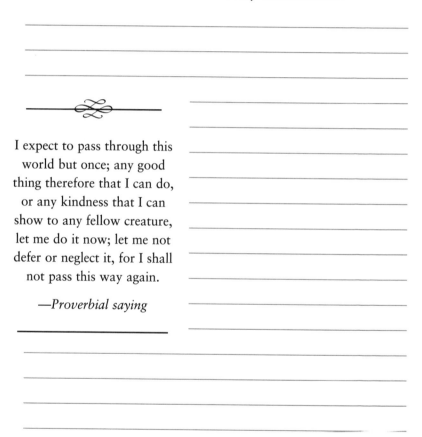

I expect to pass through this world but once; any good thing therefore that I can do, or any kindness that I can show to any fellow creature, let me do it now; let me not defer or neglect it, for I shall not pass this way again.

—*Proverbial saying*

TAKEAWAY TRUTH: Today, I will return good for evil. I will respond in kindness and mercy so I can help heal wounded hearts.

DAY 4:

OPEN HEARTS, OPEN HANDS

KEY TRUTH: People everywhere are desperate to experience the love and compassion of our God.

EVERYWHERE YOU GO THESE DAYS, PEOPLE ARE HURTING AND discouraged; many have broken dreams. They've made mistakes, and now their lives are a mess. They need to feel God's compassion and His unconditional love. They don't need someone to judge and criticize them, or to tell them what they're doing wrong. (In most cases, they already know that!) They need someone to bring hope and healing, someone to show God's mercy. Really, they're looking for a friend, someone who will be there to encourage them, who will take the time to listen to their story and genuinely care.

More than any other human attribute, I believe our world is crying out for people with compassion, people who love unconditionally, people who will take some time to help their fellow sojourners on this planet.

We're all so busy. We each have our own priorities and important plans and agendas. Often, our attitude is: *I don't want to be inconvenienced. Don't bother me with your problems. I've got enough problems of my own.* But the Scripture says, "If anyone . . . sees his brother and fellow believer in need, yet closes his heart of compassion against him, how can the love of God live and remain in him?" (1 John 3:17 AMP). Interesting, isn't it? God's Word implies that we all have a heart of compassion, but the question is whether it is opened or closed.

When God puts love and compassion in your heart toward someone, He's offering you an opportunity to make a difference in that person's life. You must learn to follow that love. Don't ignore it. Act on it. Somebody needs what you have.

CONSIDER THIS: God knows what He's doing. He knows who's hurting. He knows who's at the end of their rope. If you will follow that flow of love and compassion wherever it leads, you may be the answer to a desperate, lonely person's prayer. You may not fully realize the impact one brief phone call can have.

Let love lead you throughout life. Don't ever ignore that feeling of compassion inside you. Learn to follow the flow of God's divine love. He will direct your paths and show you where and how to express His love.

Has God been prompting you about someone recently, someone you've not thought about for a while? Are there relationships you can help mend? Are there lonely, elderly, struggling people in your life? List their names in the space below and consider ways you could help.

_____

_____

_____

_____

_____

_____

_____

_____
              ———❧———

_____
           We make a living by what

_____
           we get, we make a life by

_____
               what we give.

_____
         —*Winston Churchill*

_____

_____

_____

WHAT THE SCRIPTURES SAY

This is the commandment, as you have heard from the beginning, that you continue to walk in love [guided by it and following it].

—*2 John 6* AMP

Be devoted to one another in brotherly love. Honor one another above yourselves.

—*Romans 12:10* NIV

A PRAYER FOR TODAY

Father, how good You are to me! How continually kind, merciful, and gracious You are. You've blessed me with family and friends, and You gently guide my thoughts toward those whose lives I might bless with an encouraging word or some small act of kindness. Father, I want to live a compassionate, passionate life. I want to please You by living a life of generosity and mercy. Lead me and move me. Shape my heart to be more like Yours. And I will be thankful.

To ease another's heartache is
to forget one's own.

—*Abraham Lincoln*

TAKEAWAY TRUTH: Today, I will keep my heart of compassion open.

DAY 5:

THE SEED MUST LEAD

KEY TRUTH: You can't rob God and expect Him to bless you at the same time.

ALL THROUGH THE BIBLE, WE FIND THE PRINCIPLE OF SOWING and reaping. Just as a farmer must plant some seed if he hopes to reap the harvest, we too must plant some good seed in the fields of our families, our careers, businesses, and personal relationships.

What if the farmer decided that he didn't really feel like planting, that he was tired, so he "felt led" to sit around and hope that the harvest would come in? He'd be waiting around his whole life! No, he must get the seed in the ground. That's the principle God established. In the same way, if we want to reap good things, we must sow some good seeds. Notice, we reap what we sow. If you want to reap happiness, then you have to sow some "happiness" seeds by making other people happy. If you want to reap financial blessings, you must sow financial seeds in the lives of others. If you want to reap friendships, you should sow a seed and be a friend. The seed always has to lead.

The reason many people are not growing is because they are not sowing. They are living self-centered lives. Unless they change their focus and start reaching out to others, they will probably remain in that condition.

Some people say, "I've got a lot of problems. I don't care about sowing seeds. I want to know how I can get out of my mess." This *is* how you can get out of your mess. If you want God to solve your problems, help solve someone else's problem. Get some seed in the ground!

CONSIDER THIS: Maybe, like Isaac back in Genesis, you are in some sort of famine today. It could be a financial famine; or maybe you're simply famished for friends. Possibly, you need a physical healing. Perhaps you need peace in your home. Whatever the need, one of the best things you can do is to get your mind off yourself and help meet someone else's need. If you're down and discouraged today, don't sit around feeling sorry for yourself. Go find somebody to cheer up. Sow some seeds of happiness. That's the way to receive a harvest.

Can you point to a time when someone sowed a seed of kindness and compassion in your life? Think about how that act of compassion changed your day, your situation, your attitude. Write about what it meant to you in the space below:

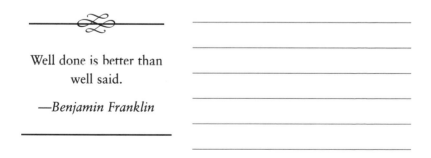

Well done is better than well said.

—*Benjamin Franklin*

_____

_____

_____

_____

_____

_____

_____ —— ❦ ——

> Generosity is a matter of the heart and not the pocketbook.
>
> —*Fred P. Corson*

_____

_____

_____

WHAT THE SCRIPTURES SAY

Whatever a man sows, that and that only is what he will reap.

—*Galatians 6:7 AMP*

Isaac sowed in that land, and reaped in the same year a hundredfold; and the LORD blessed him.

—*Genesis 26:12 NKJV*

A PRAYER FOR TODAY

Lord, I believe You when You say that when we plant and sow and water the lives of others, our own lives grow abundantly. Help me to be more "seed-oriented" than "need-oriented," not focusing on what I lack, but on how I can bless others. I believe that You will refresh my life, even in the driest, dreariest seasons, when I live to bless others. God, I trust You to meet my needs. I trust You to do more than I can ask or even think. Thank You for giving me opportunities to sow seeds of kindness into the lives of others.

It is possible to give without loving, but it is impossible to love without giving.

—*Richard Braunstein*

TAKEAWAY TRUTH: I've made up my mind. I'm going to be a giver. I'm going to make my life a garden, sowing seeds of God's love every day.

DAY 6:

GET GOD'S ATTENTION

KEY TRUTH: Do something extraordinary as an expression of your faith.

THE OTHER DAY SOMEBODY WROTE ME AND SAID, "JOEL, I SURE like that tie you wore last week on television." So I just boxed it up and I mailed it to him. I thought, *That is too good an opportunity to pass up.* (Now, don't write me and tell me you like my suit, or the car I drive. That's cheating. You know my secret!)

You may say, "Joel, I could never do something like that, giving something to somebody simply because they paid me a compliment."

Fine, but do what you can do. You can give somebody a ride. You can call somebody and encourage them. You could go to the grocery store for an elderly person. You can do something. Start today!

Learn to stretch your faith. Do something out of the ordinary. If you want an extraordinary harvest, sow an extraordinary seed. Instead of sitting at home watching TV every night, why not spend some of that time doing something good for somebody else? Instead of going out to eat at an expensive restaurant, why not save that money, and sow it as a seed? If you normally give 10 percent of your income, stretch your faith a bit and give 11 percent. Get a little more seed in the ground and watch what God will do.

The Scripture says, "Whatever measure you use to give—large or small—will be used to measure what is given back to you" (Luke 6:38 TLB). In other words, if you give with a teaspoon, it's going to be given back to you with a teaspoon. If you give with a shovel, it's going to be given back with a shovel. And if you give with a dump truck, you're going to get dump-truck loads of blessings in your life!

CONSIDER THIS: The Scripture is not ambiguous about this matter. It says, "In everything you do, put God first, and he will direct you and crown your efforts with success" (Proverbs 3:6 TLB). If you want to prosper in your finances, put God first. If you want to prosper in your business, put God first. When you honor God, God will always honor you. And it's interesting that the only place in the Bible God tells us to *prove* Him—which means to test Him, or check Him out—is in the area of our finances. If you will be faithful and show God that you're trustworthy with what you have right now, there's no limit to what God will do in your life.

In the space below, reflect on Proverbs 3:6 and what it means (or might mean) in your life today.

_____

_____

_____

_____

_____

No one is useless in his world
who lightens the burden of it
for anyone else.

—*Charles Dickens*

_____

WHAT THE SCRIPTURES SAY

Trust in the Lord and do good. Then you will live safely in the
land and prosper.

—*Psalm 37:3* NLT

He who sows sparingly will also reap sparingly, and he who
sows bountifully will also reap bountifully.

—*2 Corinthians 9:6* NKJV

A PRAYER FOR TODAY

Father, I don't want to rob from You. I don't want to take
credit for the blessings in my life. All of it comes from You.

Forgive me for the times I've been selfish with what You've given me. I want to honor You with my finances, even beyond the 10 percent You've asked of me. I want to be extravagant in my love for You and in my love for others. Help me to follow Your lead, to honor You by being faithful with what You've given me.

You cannot do a kindness too soon, for you never know how soon it will be too late.

—*Ralph Waldo Emerson*

TAKEAWAY TRUTH: I will honor God with my finances. I will not only give what is expected, I will give that which is unexpected, especially to those who don't have the resources to do something similar for me. I will start today.

DAY 7:

SOWING AND GROWING

KEY TRUTH: If God has given you joy, share it with somebody else.

THE DEAD SEA IS ONE OF THE MOST FASCINATING BODIES OF water on Earth. The water is so dense, due to the high mineral content, even a nonswimmer can stay afloat. A human being can actually sit down in the water, and read a newspaper without sinking.

Bus tours of the area stop long enough for skeptical or adventurous tourists to take a dip. Problem is, when you come out of the water, nobody wants to sit next to you! The water reeks with a wretched smell.

Fed by Israel's Jordan River, the Dead Sea has no outlet. All of the fresh water flowing into it becomes stagnant. While it is interesting to look at and fascinating to study, the water is undrinkable, polluted, and putrid.

That is a good picture of a person who lives selfishly, who is a taker but not a giver. God did not create us to be a reservoir that only collects. He created us to be a river that's constantly flowing. When we live selfishly, always receiving, always taking, but never giving, we become stagnant and polluted. Putting it bluntly, our lives will start to stink. We'll go around with a sour attitude; we'll be no fun to be around, always irritable, and hard to get along with. And all because nothing is flowing out of us. Yes, God wants to pour good things into your life, but if you want to live your best life now, you must learn to allow those good things to flow through you to others. As you do, your supply will be replenished and your life will maintain its freshness.

CONSIDER THIS: When you give, you are storing up God's goodness and His favor so in your time of need, you'll have a great harvest out of which God can "draw" to meet your need. You may not have any pressing needs today. That's great! But don't let that stop you from giving. You need to prepare for the future. When you do have a need, God will be right there to help you out. Giving is similar to taking a preventive medicine. We are storing up God's goodness.

In the space below, reflect on various needs in your life, the things you are trusting God to provide. Then at the bottom write "Because of my generosity, God will move heaven and earth to make sure that I am taken care of."

_____

_____

_____

_____

_____

_____

_____

_____

_____

_____

_____

_____

_____

_____

_____

_____

_____

_____

> Always do right; this will gratify some people and astonish the rest.
>
> —*Mark Twain*

WHAT THE SCRIPTURES SAY

Give generously, for your gifts will return to you later. Divide your gifts among many, for in the days ahead you yourself may need much help.

—*Ecclesiastes 11:1–2* TLB

Though they have been going through much trouble and hard times, their wonderful joy and deep poverty have overflowed in rich generosity.

—*2 Corinthians 8:2* NLT

A PRAYER FOR TODAY

Father, I pray that You'll make my life a river—a constantly flowing river of mercy and kindness to others. Use me to bring hope and joy to those who need it most. I trust You to meet my needs, so I am free to focus on helping meet the needs of others. Whether I have a little or a lot, what I have I give back to You.

—————————————————

—————————————————

—————————————————

—————————————————

⁓

God has given us two hands—one to receive with and the other to give with. We are not cisterns made for hoarding. We are channels made for sharing.

—*Billy Graham*

TAKEAWAY TRUTH: The generosity and joy I share with others will come back to me in my time of need.

STEP SEVEN:

Choose to Be Happy

DAY 1:

GOD SEES YOUR GIFTS

KEY TRUTH: God is keeping a record of every good deed you've ever done.

IN THE BIBLE THERE'S A STORY ABOUT A ROMAN ARMY CAPTAIN named Cornelius. The Bible says that he was a good man who prayed often and gave generously to the poor. Cornelius and his family became the first recorded Gentile household to receive the good news, and to experience salvation after the resurrection of Jesus.

Why was he chosen? Why did God pick him for such an honor? The Scripture itself explains: "An angel of God . . . said to him, 'Your prayers and your alms have come for a memorial before God'" (Acts 10:3–4 NKJV). The Living Bible translation says, "Your prayers and charities have not gone unnoticed by God!" Friend, don't let anyone convince you that giving doesn't make a difference. The reason Cornelius was chosen was because of his giving spirit.

In the same way, when we give, it gets God's attention. I'm not suggesting that we can buy miracles. I'm not saying you have to pay God to meet your needs, but I am saying God sees your gifts. He sees your acts of kindness. Every time you help someone, God sees. And as with Cornelius, it pleases God when you give, and He will pour out His favor in a new way in your life.

CONSIDER THIS: In your time of need, put some action behind your prayers. If you are praying for a promotion at work, sow some seed. Do more than pray. Why don't you do as Cornelius, and go out and feed the poor, or do something to get that seed in the ground? Your gifts will go up as a memorial before God.

Perhaps you are hoping to restore your marriage or improve some other relationship, or to buy a new home or get out of debt. Sow a special seed that relates to your specific need. We can't buy God's goodness, but like Cornelius, we can exercise our faith through giving.

In the space below, reflect on the gifts God has given you, gifts you can use to sow seeds of kindness into the lives of others.

_____

_____

_____

_____

_____

_____

_____

_____

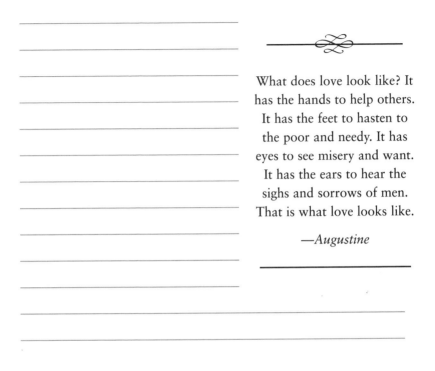

What does love look like? It has the hands to help others. It has the feet to hasten to the poor and needy. It has eyes to see misery and want. It has the ears to hear the sighs and sorrows of men. That is what love looks like.

—*Augustine*

WHAT THE SCRIPTURES SAY

Cheerful givers are the ones God prizes. God is able to make it up to you by giving you everything you need and more, so that there will not only be enough for your own needs, but plenty left over to give joyfully to others.

—*2 Corinthians 9:7–8* TLB

The gift of God is eternal life in Christ Jesus our Lord.

—*Romans 6:23* NIV

A PRAYER FOR TODAY

Lord, I know Your love for me is unconditional and You have blessed me with so many things I don't deserve, things I couldn't possibly earn, no matter how many good deeds I might do. I thank You for that and for the peace of knowing that You will always love and care for me. I want to live my faith in an extraordinary way, to live so generously that You can't help but notice my life as an offering of worship.

The real problem is not why some pious, humble, believing people suffer, but why some do not.

—*C. S. Lewis*

TAKEAWAY TRUTH: God sees my gifts, and when I am generous with others, He is even more generous with me.

DAY 2:

HAPPINESS IS A CHOICE

KEY TRUTH: Happiness is a decision you make, not an emotion you feel.

HAVING WORKED THROUGH THE FIRST SIX STEPS TO LIVING your best life now, you may be tempted to think your best life is still a long way off. Actually, nothing could be farther from the truth. Your best life starts today! God wants you to enjoy your life right now. The seventh step to enjoying your best life now is to choose to be happy today! You don't have to wait for everything to be perfectly straightened out in your family or with your business, or for all your problems to be solved. You don't have to forgo happiness until you lose weight, break an unhealthy habit, or accomplish all your goals. No, God wants you to be happy right where you are, right now.

Happiness is a choice. You may be going through tough times, or you may have major obstacles in your path, all of which give you good reason to be unhappy or upset. But being unhappy won't change anything for the better. Being negative and sour isn't going to improve anything, either. You might as well choose to be happy and enjoy your life! When you do that, not only will you feel better, but your faith will cause God to show up and work wonders in your life. God knows that we have difficulties, struggles, and challenges. But it was never His intention for us to live one day "on cloud nine," and the next day down in the dumps, defeated and depressed because we have problems. No, God wants us to live consistently. He wants us to enjoy every single day of our lives.

Learn to live one day at a time. By an act of your will, choose to start enjoying your life right now. Life is too short not to enjoy every single day. Enjoy your family, your friends, your health, your work—enjoy everything in your life. Happiness is a decision you make, not an emotion you feel. Certainly there are times in all our lives when bad things happen, or when things don't turn out as we had hoped. But that's when we must make a decision to be happy in spite of our circumstances.

CONSIDER THIS: The Bible says we are like a mist, a vapor, here for a moment, then we're gone (see James 4:14). Life is flying by, so don't waste another moment of your precious time being angry, unhappy, or worried. The psalmist said, "This is the day the LORD has made; we will rejoice and be glad in it" (118:24 NKJV). Notice that he didn't say, "Tomorrow, I will be happy." He didn't say, "Next week, when I don't have so many problems, then I'm going to rejoice." No, he said *this* is the day. This is the day that God wants you to be happy.

List seven things, right off the top of your head, that you have to be happy about:

_____

_____

_____

Happiness is contagious.
Be a carrier!

—*Robert Orben*

WHAT THE SCRIPTURES SAY

A happy heart makes the face cheerful . . . The cheerful heart
has a continual feast.

—*Proverbs 15:13, 15 NIV*

He will yet fill your mouth with laughing, and your lips with
rejoicing.

—*Job 8:21 NKJV*

A PRAYER FOR TODAY

God, I know You made me who I am on purpose. This is
Your plan, and You have given me what I have to work with.
I'm not going to complain or get negative. I'm not going to go
through life wishing things were different, wishing I was some-

body else. Father, I'm going to take what You've given me, and I'm going to make the most of it. I'm going to be happy with who You made me to be. I'm going to enjoy my life in spite of my shortcomings.

Happiness is inward, and not outward; and so, it does not depend on what we have, but on what we are.

—*Henry Van Dyke*

TAKEAWAY TRUTH: I'm not perfect, but I'm going to bloom where God planted me—in colorful, vivid and amazing ways! I am grateful for who I am, and I choose to be happy!

DAY 3:

TRUST = CONTENTMENT

KEY TRUTH: Quit questioning God and start trusting Him.

SOME PEOPLE ARE CONVINCED THAT LIFE IS SIMPLY A SERIES OF problems to be solved. The sooner they get through with this problem, the sooner they will be happy. But the truth is, after you successfully make it through this problem, there will be another problem to face. And after you overcome that obstacle, there will be something else to overcome. There's always another mountain to climb. That's why it is important to enjoy the journey, not just the destination. In this world, we will never arrive at a place where everything is perfect and we have no more challenges. As admirable as setting goals and reaching them may be, you can't get so focused on accomplishing your goals that you make the mistake of not enjoying where you are right now.

Big events will not keep you happy. They may make you happy for a while, but after that wears off, like an addict looking for a fix, you're going to need something else. Maybe you have allowed yourself to slip into the habit of waiting for everything to be calm, serene, and settled before you lighten up and grant yourself permission to enjoy your life. You're waiting for your problems to be solved. You're waiting for your spouse to become more spiritual. You're waiting for your child to change, for your business to grow, or for your mortgage to be paid off. Why not be happy right now? Don't go many years down the road and then, tragically too late, realize that one or even a series of events or achievements did not bring you lasting happiness. Appreciate today. Enjoy life's journey. These are the good old days. Twenty years from now, hopefully, you will look back and say, "That was a great time in my life!"

CONSIDER THIS: The apostle Paul wrote more than half the New Testament while incarcerated, often in tiny prison cells not much bigger than a small bathroom. Some historians and Bible commentators believe the sewage system of that day ran right through one of the dungeons in which he was imprisoned. Some commentaries state that it's possible he could have written some of the great passages of what we now know as the New Testament standing in raw sewage that at times came all the way to his waist. Yet Paul wrote such amazing faith-filled words as, "I can do all things through Christ who strengthens me" (Philippians 4:13 NKJV); "Thanks be to God, who always leads us in triumph in Christ" (2 Corinthians 2:14 NASB); and "Rejoice in the Lord always. I will say it again: Rejoice!" (Philippians 4:4 NIV).

In your difficulties, when things aren't going your way, instead of having a pity party and thinking about how unfair life is treating you, instead of feeling sorry for yourself, make a decision to rejoice in the Lord. Choose to be happy! Choose to stay full of joy.

In the space below, list three specific challenges you are

presently facing, and then name at least one specific reason to rejoice in the Lord for each challenge:

_____

_____

_____

_____

_____

_____

_____

_____

_____

_____

_____

_____

> True contentment is a real, even active virtue—not only affirmative but creative. It is the power of getting out of any situation all there is in it.
>
> —*G. K. Chesterton*

WHAT THE SCRIPTURES SAY

The joy of the LORD is your strength.

—*Nehemiah 8:10* NIV

A merry heart does good, like medicine.

—*Proverbs 17:22* NKJV

I have learned how to be content (satisfied to the point where I am not disturbed or disquieted) in whatever state I am.

—*Philippians 4:11* AMP

A PRAYER FOR TODAY

Father, I know that You have me in this place in my life for a purpose. The problems I'm experiencing help me to see Your hand at work each day. Help me to make the choice to trust You and be happy, despite my circumstances. Teach me. Push me. Stretch me. And help me respond faithfully and with a positive outlook. I trust You with my life. You are the source of my contentment. I will depend on You to guide my steps.

The Good Lord can make
you anything you want to be,
but you have to put
everything in His hands.

—*Mahalia Jackson*

TAKEAWAY TRUTH: God is in control. He has my best interests at heart. He has me right where He can best use me. He's directing my steps.

DAY 4:

THE CENTER OF THE MARK

KEY TRUTH: God doesn't bless mediocrity. God blesses excellence.

FOR MANY PEOPLE, MEDIOCRITY IS THE NORM; THEY WANT TO do as little as they possibly can and still get by. But God did not create us to be mediocre or average. He doesn't want us to just barely get by, or to do what everybody else is doing. No, God has called us to be a cut above. He's called us to stand out in the crowd, to be people of excellence and integrity. Indeed, the only way to be truly happy is to live with excellence and integrity. Any hint of compromise will taint our greatest victories or our grandest achievements.

What does it mean to be a person of excellence and integrity?

A person of excellence and integrity goes the extra mile to do what's right. He keeps his word even when it's difficult. People of excellence arrive at work on time. They give their employers a full day's work; they don't leave early or call in sick when they are not. When you have an excellent spirit, it shows up in the quality of your work and the attitude with which you do it.

God doesn't bless mediocrity. He blesses excellence. The Scripture says, "Whatever you do, work at it with all your heart, as working for the Lord, not for men, since you know that you will receive an inheritance from the Lord as a reward" (Colossians 3:23–24 NIV). Notice, whatever we do, we should give it our best effort, and do it as if we were doing it for God. If we'll work with that standard in mind, God promises to reward us.

If you want to live your best life now, start aiming for excellence and integrity in your life, doing a little bit more than you are required to do. Start making the more excellent choices in every area of life, even the mundane.

CONSIDER THIS: You may be in a situation today where everyone around you is compromising their integrity or taking the easy way out. Don't let that rub off on you. Be the one to have an excellent spirit. Be the one to stand out in the crowd.

You represent God through the way you live, the way you take care of yourself and your possessions, and the way you interact with others. In the space below, note three areas of your life in which you could make better choices. How could you aim for excellence in those areas?

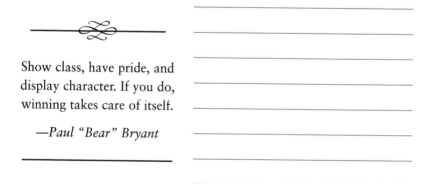

Show class, have pride, and display character. If you do, winning takes care of itself.

—*Paul "Bear" Bryant*

—————

Obstacles cannot crush me.
Every obstacle yields to stern
resolve. He who is fixed
to a star does not change
his mind.

—*Leonardo da Vinci*

WHAT THE SCRIPTURES SAY

Whoever can be trusted with very little can also be trusted with much.

—*Luke 16:10* NIV

The steps of a good man are ordered by the LORD.

—*Psalm 37:23* NKJV

Since the Lord is directing our steps, why try to understand everything that happens along the way?

—*Proverbs 20:24* TLB

A PRAYER FOR TODAY

Father, I want to be a person of excellence. The kind of person who consistently does the right thing, whether anyone is looking or not. The kind of person who shows up on time, takes good care of myself and deals honestly with others—all as a reflection of my Father in heaven. Help me to make wise decisions, always being mindful that I am Your ambassador.

_____

Life is a mirror. If you frown at it, it frowns back; if you smile, it returns the greeting.

—*William Makepeace Thackeray*

TAKEAWAY TRUTH: Taking one day at a time, I will aim for excellence in every area of my life.

DAY 5:

INTEGRITY PAYS

KEY TRUTH: Subtle compromises of integrity will keep you from God's best.

GOD WANTS US TO BE PEOPLE OF EXCELLENCE AND INTEGRITY. If you don't have integrity, you will never reach your highest potential. Integrity is the foundation on which a truly successful life is built. Every time you compromise, every time you are less than honest, you are causing a slight crack in your foundation. If you continue compromising, that foundation will never be able to hold what God wants to build. You'll never have lasting prosperity if you don't first have integrity. Oh, you may enjoy some temporary success, but you'll never see the fullness of God's favor unless you take the high road and make the more excellent choices. On the other hand, God's blessings will overtake us if we settle for anything less than living with integrity.

Of course, we all want to prosper in life. But the real question is: Are we willing to pay the price of doing the right thing? It's not always easy. Are we paying our honest debts? Are we being above board in our business decisions? Are we treating other people with respect and honor? Are we being true to our word? Integrity and prosperity are flip sides of the same coin. You can't have one without the other.

God may be reminding you about paying a bill that you've swept under the rug. Maybe you need to work on getting to the office on time consistently; maybe you know you should be more truthful in that business deal. Start making things right. Step up to a higher level of integrity in those areas. God is calling us out of mediocrity and into excellence.

A person of integrity says what he means and he means what he says. People should not have to try to figure out what you *really* mean. Be straightforward in your statements and conversations. Integrity is more than not telling a lie. A person of integrity will not deceive or mislead in any way. Often it's easy to tell part of the truth while conveniently leaving out something we know might have a negative impact. That is not speaking with integrity. We need to be open and honest even when it's difficult.

People of excellence do what's right because it is right, not because somebody is forcing them to do it.

CONSIDER THIS: Friend, there are a lot of things you can get away with in life and still be acceptable in society's eyes. You can compromise your personal integrity, or that of your company; you can cheat people or be dishonest. You can lie, steal, and compromise your morals, and you can cut corners here and there. But the question is: How high do you want to go? How much of God's favor do you want to see? How much do you want God to use you? God cannot promote you, He cannot bless you, if you are not living in integrity.

In the space below, think about these questions and respond honestly, from the heart:

———⁂———

History is made at night.
Character is what you are in
the dark.

—*Lord John Whorfin*

WHAT THE SCRIPTURES SAY

He holds victory in store for the upright, he is a shield to those
whose walk is blameless.

—*Proverbs 2:7 NIV*

Show me Your ways, O LORD; teach me Your paths.

—*Psalm 25:4 NKJV*

A PRAYER FOR TODAY

Lord, I thank You for promising victory for those who live
uprightly, for those who seek to honor You by living a life of integrity. Help me not to compromise, not to back down or cut
corners just because I can. Help me to make decisions that
honor You. Help me to give 110 percent at work, to go above

and beyond duty. Not in expectation of blessing or reward, but because it pleases You.

———————— ⁂ ————————

Do all the good you can, by all the means you can, in all the ways you can, in all the places you can, at all the times you can, to all the people you can, as long as ever you can.

—*John Wesley*

TAKEAWAY TRUTH: I will take responsibility for my own actions and decisions. I will be a person of excellence—the same both in private and in public.

DAY 6:

———❧———

THIS IS THE LIFE!

KEY TRUTH: God's people should be the happiest people on earth!

Living your best life now is living with enthusiasm and being excited about the life God has given you. It is believing for more good things in the days ahead, but it is also living in the moment and enjoying it to the hilt!

Let's not be naive. The pressures of modern life constantly threaten to take a toll on our enthusiasm, causing it to quickly evaporate if it is not continually replenished. You probably know some people who have lost their passion. They've lost their zest for life. Once they were excited about the future. They were excited about their dreams, but they've lost their fire.

Perhaps even in your own life, you've seen evidence of dwindling enthusiasm. Maybe at one time you were excited about your marriage. You were deeply in love, so full of passion, but now your marriage has become stale and stagnant. Or maybe you were excited about your job. You loved going to work, but recently it's become dull, routine, and boring. Maybe at one time you were excited about serving God. You couldn't wait to get to church. You loved reading your Bible, praying, and spending time with fellow believers. But lately you've been thinking, *I don't know what's wrong with me. I don't have any drive. I don't have any passion. I'm just going through the motions.*

The truth is, much of life is routine, and we can become stagnant if we're not careful. We need to stir ourselves up, to replenish our supply of God's good gifts on a daily basis. Like the Israeli people in the wilderness who had to gather God's miraculous provisions of manna afresh each morning, we, too, cannot get by on yesterday's supply. We need fresh enthusiasm each day. The word *enthusiasm* derives from two Greek words, *en theos*, which mean "inspired by God." Our lives need to be inspired, infused, filled afresh, with God's goodness every day.

CONSIDER THIS: We should be so excited and so full of joy that other people will want what we have. Ask yourself, "Is the way I'm living attractive and contagious? Will my attitudes, the words I speak, my expressions, the way I handle challenges and setbacks, cause anybody to want what I have?"

In the space below, list five words that honestly describe your attitude/outlook on life (For instance: *upbeat, discouraged, positive, enthusiastic,* etc.). Are you simply going through the motions, surviving the day to day, or are you generally positive and enthusiastic about your life? Would these characteristics in you attract people to you (and to your God)?

_____

_____

_____

_____

The most wasted of all days is one without laughter.

—E. E. Cummings

WHAT THE SCRIPTURES SAY

Never lag in zeal and in earnest endeavor; be aglow and burning with the Spirit, serving the Lord.

—*Romans 12:11* AMP

Fan into flames the spiritual gift God gave you.

—*2 Timothy 1:6* NLT

A PRAYER FOR TODAY

Lord, if it were not for Your goodness, I might not even be here today. I know You are at work in my life, and I know there's no better life than life in You! Knowing this, I'm going to quit looking at what's wrong and start thinking about what's right in my life. Help me, Father, to get up each day expecting good things.

You've promised Your favor and protection and blessing in my life, so I'm going to believe what You've said. I'm going to live my life with excitement and enthusiasm, even when my circumstances aren't the greatest. Because You are the greatest!

If no one ever took risks, Michelangelo would have painted the Sistine floor.

—*Neil Simon*

TAKEAWAY TRUTH: It doesn't matter what anybody else does or doesn't do, I'm going to live my life with enthusiasm! I'm going to stay on fire. I'm going to be aglow. I'm going to be passionate about seeing my dreams come to pass.

DAY 7:

YOUR BEST LIFE NOW

KEY TRUTH: God has great things in store for you.

TOO OFTEN, AS TIME GOES BY, WE TAKE FOR GRANTED WHAT God has done for us. We get up in the morning and say, "Well, that's just my wife (or husband). No big deal. Sorry, honey, I don't have time to give you a hug. I'm in a hurry . . ." What we once regarded as a miracle has now become commonplace. We've grown cool to it; we take what we have for granted.

But the good news is, that fire can be rekindled. In your marriage, in your career, in your personal relationships, in your life! If you will initiate the changes you've learned about in this book, the excitement will come back. Rekindle that fire. Don't take life for granted.

Don't take for granted the greatest gift of all God has given to you—Himself! Don't allow your relationship with Him to become stale, or your appreciation for His goodness to become common. Get your fire back. Fan the flame more than ever. Live with enthusiasm. Whatever you do, do it for Him, with your whole heart.

Friend, God doesn't want you to drag through life defeated and depressed. No matter what you've been through, no matter whose fault it was, no matter how impossible your situation may look, the good news is, God wants to turn it around and restore everything that has been stolen from you. He wants to restore your marriage, your family, your career. He wants to restore those broken dreams. He wants to restore your joy and give you a peace and happiness you've never known before. Most of all, He wants to restore your relationship with Him. God wants you to live a satisfied life.

God is in the long-term restoration business. He has great things in store for you!

CONSIDER THIS: Hold on to that new, enlarged vision of victory that God has given to you. Start expecting things to change in your favor. Dare to boldly declare that you are standing strong against the forces of darkness. You will not settle for a life of mediocrity!

Raise your level of expectancy. It's our faith that activates the power of God. Let's quit limiting Him with our small-minded thinking, and start believing Him for bigger and better things. Remember, if you obey God and are willing to trust Him, you will have the best this life has to offer—and more! Make a decision that from this day forward, you are going to be excited about the life God has for you.

Enlarge your vision. Develop a healthy self-image. Discover the power of your thoughts and words. Let go of the past. Stand strong against opposition and adversity. Live to give. Make the choice to be happy. And God will take you places you've never dreamed. You will be living your best life now!

_____

_____

_____

_____

_____

_____

_____

_____

_____

_____

—⟨⟩—

One hundred percent of the
shots you don't take
don't go in.

—*Wayne Gretzky*

_____

_____

_____

_____

_____

WHAT THE SCRIPTURES SAY

If you are willing and obedient, you will eat the best from the
land.

—*Isaiah 1:19 NIV*

God loves a cheerful giver.

—*2 Corinthians 9:7 NASB*

A PRAYER FOR TODAY

Father, I give You my life, my dreams, my desires, my problems,
my past, my fears, my doubts, my weaknesses—everything I have,

I give to You. Lord, You are so good to me. I know You have planned my life to be so much larger and fulfilling than I could ever have planned for myself. You are the source of everything good and true in this life. I want to live my best life now, not to-morrow, not next year. *Now.* And I believe, with all my heart, all my soul, and all my mind that You have made me to live that way! Thank You, Lord, for all You've done and for all You have in store for me!

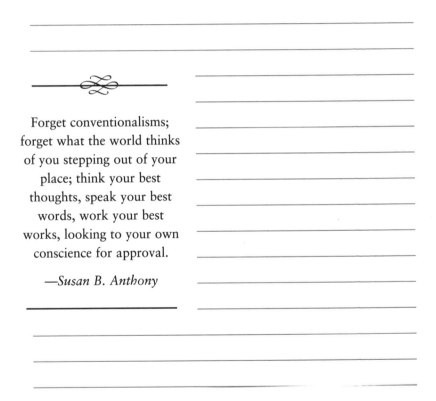

Forget conventionalisms; forget what the world thinks of you stepping out of your place; think your best thoughts, speak your best words, work your best works, looking to your own conscience for approval.

—*Susan B. Anthony*

TAKEAWAY TRUTH: My faith—my obedience and my willingness to trust—activates the power of God. My best life starts now!